D0684205

Parker J. Palmer has been senior associate at the Washington Center for Metropolitan Studies, co-founder of the Institute for Public Life, professor of sociology at Georgetown University, and dean of studies at Pendle Hill, the Quaker community and adult study center. His previous book is *The Promise of Paradox.*

"In *The Company of Strangers,* Palmer attempts to sketch a vision, stimulate imaginations, encourage the beginning of a movement. His goal: the rebuilding of America's public life . . . His own community experience and prayer are clearly sources of the rich variety of psychological, social and religious insights that punctuate this work. He presents them clearly and provocatively, avoiding sexist language with simplicity and grace."   —*America*

"If you preach each Sunday, or are looking for a renewal in your church's mission program, *The Company of Strangers* will make an excellent resource."
                                                        —*Pacific Theological Review*

"Without a doubt, the best book I've read in the past year . . . The emphasis throughout is positive and creative, with numerous suggestions on what to do and how to do it."   —*Mennonite Weekly Review*

"Palmer's work should be collateral reading in courses on American religion and society and seminars on professional ethics."—*Religious Studies Review*

"An idealistic yet sensible work, highly recommended."   —*Library Journal*

"Only those who believe the world is coming to a quick end should avoid this book. Others, who retain some degree of hopefulness, will find in it both competent exegesis and perceptive social analysis articulating that hope."
                                                                    —*Homiletic*

"In *The Company of Strangers,* Parker Palmer shows us how we can again put our faith and hope in each other and turn strangers into friends with our love."
                                                            —*Friends Journal*

Parker J. Palmer

THE COMPANY
OF STRANGERS

*Christians and the Renewal
of America's Public Life*

Foreword by
MARTIN E. MARTY

CROSSROAD · NEW YORK

93-809

1988
The Crossroad Publishing Company
370 Lexington Avenue, New York, NY 10017

Library of Congress Cataloging in Publication Data

Palmer, Parker J.
  The company of strangers.

  Includes bibliographical references.
  1. Church and the world. 2. Christians—United
States. I. Title.
BR115.W6P3   261   81-7768
ISBN 0-8245-0601-4 (pbk)

To My Mother and Father

Contents

Acknowledgments   9

Foreword   11

1 · Life Among Strangers
  An Introduction   17

2 · The Public Life
  Its Nature and Nurture   34

3 · A Spirituality of Public Life
  The Stranger as Spiritual Guide   56

4 · Private, Public, and Political
  The Vital Links   71

5 · Teaching the Public Life I
  Scarcity and Abundance   90

6 · Teaching the Public Life II
  Conflict, Compassion, and the Way of the Cross   106

7 · Practicing the Public Life
  The Congregation as Community   118

8 · Building the Public Life
  The Congregation in Mission   135

9 · Hope for the Public
  Private Contemplation and the Public Congregation   153

Notes   167

Acknowledgments

The power of public life is such that our ideas and visions are mere phantoms until they enter the public realm and receive a public response. To cross over into that life-giving but intimidating space, most of us need the prodding and support of friends. I am grateful for the chance to name some people who have done just that for me, and to thank them in public.

—Patricia Hall and Elden Jacobson, my colleagues ten years ago in the Institute for Public Life.

—Members of the Silver Spring Group Ministry (especially Robert Marston, Donald Misal, Tracy Boyer, Ronald Albaugh, John Murphy, and Marion Michael) who supported the work of the Institute, even when it didn't work.

—Robert Bellah and William L. Kolb, my teachers, from whom I learned by both word and deed about the relations of faith and society.

—The staff of the Lilly Endowment, Inc., who provided financial support to help this work along.

—The Institute for Cultural and Ecumenical Research at St. John's Abbey and University which provided a Fellowship and a splendid sabbatical, 1980–81.

—Edward W. Jones, Richard Hamilton, Carl R. Smith, and Richard L. Lancaster, ministers in the city of Indianapolis, who thoughtfully criticized and confirmed earlier versions of this manuscript.

—Many friends and Friends at Pendle Hill who have helped me understand what life in the church is all about.

—Henri Nouwen and John Mogabgab, whose cultivation of my faith and my writing has been so vital.

—Sally, Brent, Todd, and Carrie Palmer, who have lovingly borne my many contradictions, including my need to be private and sometimes cross while I urged others to be public and caring.

—Robert W. Lynn, without whom this book would not have been written. His gifts of faith, intellect, personal challenge, and affirmation, have deepened my sense of calling and my resolve to follow that call.

Nurtured by this company of family and friends, the ideas in this book now enter "the company of strangers." I like that phrase because the public life is a life shared by strangers, and the word "company" suggests the qualities our public life must have. On the one hand, a company is a group of people gathered for a common purpose—in this case, working to create a world which will sustain our finest hopes. On the other hand, the word suggests the hospitality which strangers must offer each other to achieve that common goal—as when we enjoy each other's company. And at its roots, that word reaches to the heart of the church's public ministry. "Company" comes from two Latin terms, *com* and *panis,* literally meaning "sharing bread together." This image, rich in Christian understanding from the Last Supper to last Sunday's breaking of bread, identifies the healing power the church might bring to America's divided public: God's gift of reconciliation.

Foreword

No one can credibly accuse Parker Palmer of riding a boom as he urges Christians in America to "go public." If the concept of the public is a fad, it is the least noticed fad of its time and place. If Palmer, the writer who promotes it, is playing secretary to the *Zeitgeist,* taking notes for "the spirit of the times," then these are different times than the ones whose signs most of us are able to read.

"Going private" has instead been the main trend in cultural and religious life for well over a decade and for almost a generation. In the first decades after World War II, through the Eisenhower and Kennedy-Johnson years, idealists of both political parties called people to be mindful of the public sector. The churches, whether during the revival of the fifties or in the social service and activities of the early sixties, did not lack leaders who called people to consciousness of the public order.

After the chaos of the mid-sixties, as soon as the young learned that their dreams of utopia were to be denied, the activists ran out of energy, the culturally alert were numbed in the horrors of burning cities and morally dubious overseas adventures, and a private-style *Zeitgeist* took over.

The campus for a time was the best place to look for trends, to read the spirit of the times. And people on campuses, after making a pit stop in the counterculture, found it advisable or necessary to organize their curricula and their lives for private interests. Polls of the young and the larger public alike showed Americans generally satisfied with their personal life and prospects, yet wildly apprehensive about the possibility of the culture "making it." Such paradoxes in the polls, of course, point to realities with which the nation sooner or later must cope. One cannot have it both ways: 220 million people, or at least the 60%–70% of them who think things will turn out all right for them, will not find much of anything turning out all right if the economy, politics, the arts, literature, the media, and church life all are devastated.

So we have seen people line up at economics departments' doors as they pursue the Master of Business Administration degree that is their ticket to what is left of the goodies of the good life for the short span ahead. Other professions, especially if they pay well, are alluring. There is nothing wrong with these professions. Anyone with a public interest has to hope that they will draw the best talent and energies of a generation. But, as Robert Heilbroner has observed of the seekers of security and those who surround them, everyone has been interested in personal morals, while few have cared about public morale. And a society built on competing sets of personal interests does not know how to move from there to "going public."

As in mundane life, so in affairs of the sacred, America took a turn toward the intensely private. Here one treads cautiously: people have always made use of their religious vision for private ends, and they always will and should. Religion in general and Christianity in particular set out to provide meaning and experiences that inform and ennoble lives. Our existence is precarious in the face of doubt, despair, and death, and it would be hard to trust someone who claimed to be a person of faith but lacked interest in the private dimensions of spirituality.

What was disturbing in the recent past, however, was the obsessiveness of the turning. In the face of neighborhood change, rising crime waves, and complex public policy issues, it has been tempting for us to huddle together in our cells or even to take our religion secretly in our apartments. The airport newsstand offers scores of religious books that will describe occult, cultic, and macrobiotic ways to be spiritual or have a thrill. The television ministry reaches past publics and people to locate the potential viewer or donor who is safely en-rumped on the cushions of a sofa in a room behind locked doors. The always urgent "personal journey" became a purely private search for millions, across the spectrum from the evangelical market to the mainline churches' alumni association.

Ah, but I hear you saying that things are changing: hasn't the New Christian Right suddenly entered public life? Certainly it has come to be in the public eye, as it intervenes in elections, constitutional amendment and legislative processes, and efforts to impose standards on the media. Give them credit at least for caring. But most of their activity is purely political, not public, and there is a difference, as Palmer points out in the pages ahead. Most of the Moral Majoritarians care about America because it is the last chosen training ground for evangelists who will rescue a few souls before the Second Coming. Or because America plays a role against the Gog of Russia at Armageddon. Folks are welcome to biblicial interpretations that carry them to such points, and there is no reason to single them out for special scorn if they fail to understand the public. But what they are doing is engaging in forays into the public realm. It is hard to find them caring for the public *as* public, for the people who belong to God's creation and order whether they know the name of God or not, whether they are saved or not, whether they are likely prospects for saving or not.

That is a test of the public realm: does the church only make little raids into it, or is there a theology and pattern of care for it? Is the church that set of people who, à la a W. H. Auden parody, are in effect saying, "We are all in the world to save all the other people—what all the other people are in the world for we haven't the faintest idea"?

A public outlook among Christians asks them to care for the good ordering of people who are not saved and may never be. It means having concern for arts and letters, the quality of life and its cultural dimensions, the institutions of education and the forms of politics—even if there is no direct payoff for the churches. The Bible has all kinds of ways of accounting for the validity of "the welfare of the city" to which Yahweh sends his people. Cyrus the

Persian matters as much in the divine economy as some of the (rare) saintly kings of Israel. Roman centurions come off better than disciples in most of the Gospels.

The public, in such readings, is not an accidental spillover of the people of God. The public is not a messy and hard-to-comprehend reality to disturb the coziness and clarity of God's people. The public is also a creation of God, however much the demonic may show up in its ways. The Christian believes that in Christ "the new order has already begun," the new creation is here, if only disguised and in vague outline. But it is here. The public concept does not make weeping hearts glad, does not save souls, does not answer all the questions of existence. It has its space alongside the more familiar aspects of creation and redemption.

With all that in mind, some of us have been out on lonely soil looking for traces of public concern, which is more than political, among Christians, who are not only public-minded in intention or fulfillment. For some years a colleague and I have been teaching about "public religion" in America, a strain that goes back to Benjamin Franklin and before him, to Jonathan Edwards: this *"public religion"* sees an interaction between the churches in their concern for public virtue and the "virtuous" elements in the public that share the concern. By studying Edwards through Reinhold Niebuhr or John Courtney Murray on the one hand and Abraham Lincoln and his kind on the other, we have been calling for the development of a *"public theology."* In the history of Protestantism we have seen the development of a *"public party,"* which languishes during the years of private pursuits in religion. And, with some reportorial sense and more programmatic hope, some of us have spotted what I call the *"public church,"* a new coalescence of some mainline, evangelical, and Catholic Christians.

But why advertise my courses and books while introducing another book? Simple: because in all four endeavors, I have been among those who have neglected the adjective. We have not given enough attention to the meaning of "public" itself. The dictionaries and histories give notice to the question. But we have needed a book that gives a simple "lo here!" and "lo there!" set of pointings, so we might envision what a restored public order might look like, what a public sense might achieve.

When I stumbled on an article by Parker Palmer, I found the clearest recent statement of what public means, or at least what it means for people in religion. Was there more where that little essay came from? Yes, and it is here, for that article was a kind of dry run for this book, an excerpt from the fleshed-out argument the reader will find here.

Forewords should not give away the argument or take out the suspense by providing too many clues. After setting the stage, the foreword-writer has to run to the side so that the lights can go on and the curtain can rise. Let me say only that in brief and always clear ways Parker Palmer has envisioned the outlines of a renewed public sphere. He has been practical about the ways in which people of faith might live in it and enhance it. So think of this book as a drama about the public, to be played before or, at least, read by, what I hope will be a significant public. If Palmer recruits enough people to make it possible for someone to say that public concern is a fad or a fashion, I'll be among those who smile. Not with a knowing smile, but with one that signals hope. We are going to need as much "public" as we can get in the 1980s. Here is stimulus.

MARTIN E. MARTY

1

Life Among Strangers
An Introduction

1

S hortly after finishing the first draft of this book, I went to New York City on business and took a taxi from the train to my uptown destination. The driver—a short, animated man who spoke broken but enthusiastic English—seemed eager to talk, so I asked how he liked his work. "Well," he said, "you never know who's getting into the cab, so it's a little dangerous. But you meet a lot of people. You get to know *the public.*"

With these two words he turned to look at me, speaking with an emphasis which made it clear we were on his favorite subject. The more questions I asked, the more often he turned around to underscore his point, and though we were bounding up Broadway at an alarming clip, he was soon spending more time looking back than ahead. But my terror was outweighed (just barely) by the fact that he was on my favorite subject, too, so I kept on asking questions:

> You get to know *the public.* Which teaches you a lot in life. You don't know anything if you don't know the public. You exchange ideas and you learn a lot from people. It's like going to school. Meeting all these different kinds of people, everything helps, it doesn't hurt. If you only like one kind of people, it's no good! We talk, if I have a better idea I tell them. Maybe they say yes, maybe they say no—that's how I educate myself. It makes me happy. You can't buy this kind of education. If you're with the same kind of people all the time, it's like

wearing the same suit all the time—you get sick of it. But the public
—that keeps you alive!

The man came here from Greece some fifteen years ago. It is no
coincidence that he, born into the culture which gave us our earli-
est model of public life, should live in America with an eye for
public possibilities which few native-born Americans possess. He
understands that public life is—simply and centrally—our life
among strangers, strangers with whom our lot is cast, with whom
we are interdependent whether we like it or not. And he likes it.
Without minimizing the risks and dangers of public life, he cele-
brates and makes the most of its daily blessings.

In ancient Greece, the public life was the only life worth living.
In public, free men dealt with matters of moment and mutual
concern, shaping their common destiny. For the Greeks, a young
man's entry into public life was a critical life passage. Indeed, the
word "public" finds its root in the same word which gives rise to
"puberty." Both suggest the movement into adulthood—in the one
case a physiological process, in the other a transition from private
necessities like keeping a house and making a living into the rights
and duties of civic membership.

Unfortunately, in speaking about the Greeks, I must use the
word "men" quite literally. The Greek vision was dimmed and
flawed by the fact that women and children and slaves were exclud-
ed from the public and kept in the private realm, denied the chance
to grow into full human status. Today, we continue to do battle
with various forms of slavery, with the diminishment of children,
with discrimination against women. Though progress has been
made, our very language reveals ancient prejudices: the phrase "a
public man" suggests an honored official, while "a public woman"
often means a prostitute. We still have a long way to go.

The word "private," which we often use to denote the opposite
of the public realm, literally means "to be deprived of a public life."
The private status so valued in our day, the life on which we lavish
so much energy and attention, was once regarded as a state of
deprivation. In fact, the Greek root of our word "idiot" means a

private person, one who does not hold public office, hence an ignorant individual!

I do not wish to downplay the private realm, by which I mean our relations with friends and family as well as our inward lives, our lives of solitude, reflection, prayer. Not only is private life essential to our well-being, it also contains demands and challenges as rigorous as those of the public realm. In fact, I shall argue that the renewal of private life is one of the reasons for working on the recovery of the public sphere. But today, when we seek private values at the expense of public good, the Greek way of looking at things—enlarged to include everyone—may be a healthy corrective.

Ever since the ancient Greeks, philosophers have speculated on the public and its life, but have often made these terms so distant and abstract that they seem unrelated to our daily experience. Thus, Kierkegaard could write, "Made up of . . . individuals at the moments when they are nothing, a public is a kind of gigantic something, an abstract and deserted void which is everything and nothing."[1] In our own time, "public life" has become narrowly identified with politics and governmental institutions. When we think of persons "in public life" we usually think of elected officials.

But to my taxi driver, the public is no philosophical abstraction. Nor is it a term which applies only to people engaged in politics. For him, the public is all those people, those strangers, who share his territory, who get in and out of his cab during the day, engaging his intellect, his imagination, his emotions. The public is the human world of which he is a part and on which he is dependent, a world which brings color and texture to his life, energizes and educates him, enlarges and enlivens his human experience.

The word "public" as I understand it contains a vision of our oneness, our unity, our interdependence upon one another. Despite the fact that we are strangers to one another—and will stay strangers for the most part—we occupy a common space, share common resources, have common opportunities, and must somehow learn to live together. To acknowledge that one is a member of the public is to recognize that we are members of one another.

But a vision of "the public" is not enough, and exhortation will not bring that vision into being. We need a living process to experience ourselves as a public, a process suggested by the phrase "a public life." In such a life, strangers come in daily contact, grow accustomed to each other, learn to solve the problems which the common life poses, enrich and expand each other's lives. My interest, then, is not simply in the static concept of the public but in the dynamic process known as public life. It is a process which brings us out of ourselves into an awareness of our connectedness, an awareness which is especially pronounced at moments of high public drama:

> Sometimes we recognize the public in a crisis: a President is murdered, November 22, 1963; or the threat of war, Pearl Harbor Day. Sometimes an emergency jars us out of comforting routines: a forest fire, a riot. Or the public becomes visible on those rare occasions when we are challenged by a common heritage and destiny: that August afternoon before the Lincoln Memorial and Martin Luther King, Jr., saying, "I have a dream."
>
> In these moments, that which divides us falls away and, for once, seems pitifully unimportant. And then we know, if only in part, that in some inexplicable way we actually do belong to one another, the mighty and the weak, the rich and the poor alike.[2]

Today, we live in a culture of brokenness and fragmentation. Images of individualism and autonomy are far more compelling to us than visions of unity, and the fabric of relatedness seems dangerously threadbare and frayed. Our situation has been described with force by the historian Vincent Harding:

> . . . a truly pluralistic and humane society must be undergirded and overarched by a common vision of the public good. . . . For without that capacity to see ourselves ultimately as a community, without that common basis on which community must be built, we are in danger of disintegrating into hundreds of private, warring, special interests (who will not, for instance, pay taxes to support the wellbeing of the whole; who will, for instance—at astonishingly young ages—physically attack helpless elderly citizens to grab the pittances of their social security and welfare money; who will, for instance,

pour life-destroying industrial wastes into rivers, or produce essentially poisonous products for profit alone). "Where there is no vision, the people perish. . . ."[3]

We have all but lost the vision of the public. More than ever we need the process of public life to renew our sense of belonging to one another. But in our time, along with loss of vision, opportunities for public interaction have also dwindled. We lack the facilities, the occasions, the hospitable spaces in which the public might come together to find and celebrate itself. And even more basic, we have lost the conviction that a public life is worth living.

Few of us would regard the cabdriver's life as a blessing. Most of us seek to live and work in the most private spaces possible, spaces where the public cannot intrude. We sleep, arise, and eat in the privacy of our own home (the ideal being a single-family dwelling set far apart from the neighbors); we drive to our job in the privacy of an automobile; we park in an underground garage and go to work in a space where only colleagues are allowed; then back to the auto and back to the house with little or no chance for interaction with strangers. If circumstances force us to take "public transportation" or walk the "public streets," we often find ourselves in situations so crowded, noisy, and tense that we ignore one another in hopes that conflict will not occur. In our free time, when we might mingle with the public in a park or at a sporting event, we are more inclined to watch the game on TV in the privacy of our living room.

As our public experience dwindles, we come to regard "the public" either as an empty abstraction or as a sinister, anonymous crowd whose potential for violence fills us with fear. That potential is there (as the cabbie says, "You never know who's getting into the cab, so it's a little dangerous") but we have blown it all out of proportion. As our privacy deepens and our distance from the public increases, we pay a terrible price. We lose our sense of relatedness to those strangers with whom we must share the earth; we lose our sense of comfort and at-homeness in the world. Compared to the cabdriver, our lives are sadly diminished. For the cabbie is fully at home. His appreciation of the public and his daily opportunity for public experience lead to celebration, not anxiety

—celebration of the insight and energy and connectedness which life among strangers can bring.

Despite my terror in that careening taxi, I was deeply moved by the driver's words. In them I find hope for the renewal of public life on which our individual and corporate futures depend. I confess that his words also depressed me, for they say with such clarity, brevity and force things I have labored long pages to express! Perhaps I can be forgiven. I am not blessed with Greek instincts. I have discovered the public slowly and with astonishment as only a WASP can. But I acknowledge my debt to my taxi-driving friend; I embrace him as a fellow member of the public; and I thank him for vivifying a concept which I want to offer as a focus for Christian understanding and action.

2

What has the public life to do with Christians and the church? A great deal, I think. At bottom, religion, like the public life, has to do with unity, with the overcoming of brokenness and fragmentation, with the reconciliation of that which has been estranged. The very root of the word religion means to "rebind" or "bind together," so deep does this meaning go. Both "the kingdom" and "the public" are visions of human unity, so it would seem natural that they have something to do with one another.

Of course, there are Christians who argue that the church should stay out of public life because religion and politics don't mix. I am a Christian who thinks they do mix, but that is not the point I want to make. We misunderstand public life if we equate it with politics, with the activities of government. Not only do we misunderstand it, we also strangle our sense of public possibilities. The heart of public life is simply the interaction of strangers, and that is a basic and vital human experience, not a specialized political process. Having a public life is as fundamental to our humanness, to our well-being, as having a private life; without the two halves, life cannot be whole. The God who cares about our private lives is concerned with our public lives as well. This is a God who calls us into relationship not only with family and friends, but with strangers scattered across the face of the earth, a God who says again and again, "We are all in this together."

The public life, far from being narrowly political, involves strangers who come together without elaborate institutional mechanisms—in taxis, on streetcorners, at museums and sidewalk cafes, wherever strangers meet. At its most basic level, the public life involves strangers encountering each other with no political agenda at all. In fact, the public life is "prepolitical." It is more basic than politics; it existed long before political institutions were developed and refined; and a healthy political process (at least, the process we call democracy) depends on the preexistence of a healthy public life. As important as it is to attempt to influence the government, it is even more important to renew the life of the public. Without a public which knows that it shares a common life, which is capable of feeling, thinking, debating, and deciding, politics becomes a theatre of illusion, with everyone watching the drama on stage, hoping to play some part, while the real action goes on backstage in the form of raw and unrestrained power. Without a public life, government becomes a sham, a show, an elaboration of techniques for manipulating the populace—and movements aimed at altering the government tend to become the same. Public life creates the community which both establishes legitimate government and holds it accountable to what the people want.

Even if one believes that religion and politics don't mix, there is still strong reason to believe that Christians should concern themselves with public life. For the church preaches a vision of human unity which means very little if not acted out in the public realm. Surely that vision applies to more than family and friends. Surely it is a vision which claims more than the commonality of those who think and act and look alike. Surely that vision reaches out to include those who are alien, different, strange. If so, then the church *must* incarnate its vision in public, for there and only there is the stranger to be found.

If the integrity of the church's vision depends on its public expression, the quality of public life depends on the church acting out its vision. For the church's understanding of human unity is different and deeper than the political theories which have shaped our conventional thinking about the public. In those theories, civic unity is strictly a matter of compromise and accommodation, a unity which emerges as we discover that we must yield some of our interests in order to achieve others, a unity produced by "enlightened self-interest." From a Christian point of view, this is not so much unity as it is a fragile truce, a marriage of convenience, to be dissolved whenever the self-interest of one partner requires it. The Christian is convinced of a unity which lies deeper, in our very creation and condition, a oneness which roots in the fact that—despite our strangeness to one another—we are all children of the same creator God. For the Christian, our unity is known not in politics but prayer, and is given by the grace which answers prayer. The unity sought by the church is not achieved through calculation and manipulation, but received through contemplation and vulnerability and self-giving.

3

The spiritual life, the inward life, the life of prayer faithfully pursued, will bring us back and back again to the public realm. Despite our frequent attempts to use prayer as an escape from the world, the God we meet in prayer connects us to one another—as a church and as a public. That is made abundantly clear in the story of Thomas Merton, Trappist monk and author, whose devotion to the contemplative life was as deep and relentless as any of the saints'.

Merton entered the monastery at age twenty-eight in full flight from the world. What he had seen (and been) in public repulsed and disgusted him: people, himself included, frantically running away from God toward self-degradation and destruction. So Merton retreated into one of the most private spaces imaginable—a cloistered monastery where the world is shut out. Although Merton's move was extreme, it resembles the way Christians too often use the church, as a barrier against the world, a bulwark against public life.

But in the monastery something happened to Merton, something which brought him a deep compassion for the world's people.

Monastic life gave Merton the time and space for genuine encounter with God, the opportunity to see beneath the surface into the heart of things. Through monastic discipline in meditation, contemplation, and prayer, Merton found himself drawn not farther from the world but closer and closer to the truth in whom we are one. After years of such discipline, Merton was prepared for a revelation. It came not in the monastic sanctuary but on a busy street corner in Louisville, Kentucky where the monk had made a rare trip out of the cloister to see a physician:

> In Louisville, at the corner of Fourth and Walnut, in the center of the shopping district, I was suddenly overwhelmed with the realization that I loved all those people, that they were mine and I theirs, that we could not be alien to one another even though we were total strangers. It was like waking from a dream of separateness, of spurious self-isolation in a special world, the world of renunciation and supposed holiness. . . . This sense of liberation from an illusory difference was such a relief and such a joy to me that I almost laughed out loud. And I suppose my happiness could have taken form in the words: "Thank God, thank God that I *am* like other men, that I am only a man among others."[4]

It seems odd that rigorous practice of an inward way should have led Merton back into the world, into a lively and appreciative sense of his connectedness with others; odd, because we so often think of prayer and contemplation as a private escape from wordly wars, entering into them as if we were entering a bomb shelter. What Merton learned (which we who dabble in prayer may not know) is that to follow the inward path far enough is to encounter the living God who connects us all—no matter how distant and strange we may be to each other. And Merton learned his lesson well. His revelation at Fourth and Walnut was no passing fancy. It grew and grew in his heart and in his work, making him one of our century's most compelling Christian advocates of the human community.

Merton's awakening from his "dream of separateness" is an essential part of the spiritual journey, an essential contribution which Christians can make to the renewal of the public life. The gaps and divides of the outer world are so often projections of divisions within ourselves; as our inner world is healed by spiritual discipline and experience, our public world will be healed in some measure as well. In prayer and contemplation we begin to understand that our identity is not to be found in our differences from others—in our superiorities and inferiorities—but in our common humanity. In contemplation and prayer we can cease the anxious, competitive, and ultimately violent struggle to claim a name over and above others, and relax into the good news that God names us all as brothers and sisters. Merton puts his finger on the major outcome of such an insight—joy, pure and simple joy, the joy of no longer having to struggle for a sense of separate selfhood, but of being able to proclaim, "Thank God, thank God that I *am* like other people, that I am only a person among others!"

4

If personal spiritual life is intimately related to public concern, what about the life of the church as a whole? Critics will argue that the churches, having been demoralized by the struggles of the sixties and decimated by the general trend of secularization, are the last place to look for social concern today. They will note that through the seventies the churches turned inward, becoming more interested in shielding their members from society than in trying to change that society for the better. So what are the grounds for hope that the churches can somehow contribute to the renewal of public life?

First, the grounds of faith: the church lives under a relentless divine calling to engage in the work of reconciliation—to God, to one another, and to ourselves. There is nothing about which God is more persistent than the promise that the brokenness within us and between us can and will be healed. Healing comes as a result of God's mercy and grace, not of our work. But mercy and grace are channeled as the church finds ways of more fully becoming the body of Christ, whose touch heals.

The body of Christ, in whom there is neither Jew nor Greek, slave nor free, male nor female, neither stranger nor friend: surely if we take that image seriously we are called into public life, for that is where the "other" is found. If the church were to work on the revival and reconstruction of public life, it would be undertaking a work of reconciliation. The hope that it can do so is grounded not in a naive assessment of the church's willingness to follow God's will, but in the faith that God will find ways to fulfill the promise of reconciliation—even through our recalcitrance and frailty.

The church's potential for such a ministry can be indicated by a simple factual observation: the church is the largest and most diverse voluntary association in America today. This is my second reason for hope. Only six percent of the American people claim no religious preference whatsoever, while sixty-eight percent claim membership in some church or synagogue. Forty-two percent of all American adults say they attend a service of worship during a typical week. There is no other institution which involves so large a segment of the American public on so regular a basis. What better forum in which to reach the public—or help create one?

Not only is the church large, it is also diverse, and the primary problem facing those who would help create a public is to bring unity out of diversity. Think of the wide range of people who belong to "the church" in one form or another: black Baptists, white Appalachian Pentecostalists, upper-middle-class suburban Episcopalians, blue-collar Catholic charismatics, farm-belt Swedish Lutherans. And within the average congregation there is much more diversity than our stereotypes suggest. That "upper-middle-class suburban Episcopal" congregation is far less homogeneous than it would appear on the surface. In such a congregation of any size, there is probably as wide a range of attitudes and opinions as on a university campus—suppressed, but wide. So within congregations and between them the church has the great opportunity and challenge to show how a common framework of faith can bridge vast differences in economic status, race, political orientation, social experience. Such a demonstration would provide a model for our public life.

Third, the church is in a unique position to bridge the private and the public realms, to help people walk across a gap which, in the minds of many, has become wide and forbidding. For many people (those who live in suburban isolation, for instance) the church is the only alternative to their tight circle of family and close friends, the only setting in which they might encounter the stranger. And in the church, strangers meet on safe ground, the ground of common commitment. But to serve this function, the church must resist the conventional expectation that it be an extended family, a somewhat larger version of that tight little circle. The church could become a kind of halfway house between the comforts of private life and the challenges of diversity—but only if it can stay open to strangeness and help us experience our differences within the context of a common faith.

Theologically, the church has the potential for becoming a public-private bridge because the very nature of church membership spans the two realms. The religious convictions or experiences which bring people into church membership are essentially private, matters of the hidden heart. But in joining the church an individual makes public testimony of these private matters, and has thus walked part way across the bridge whether knowingly or not. If the church could help people grow in awareness of this fact, and encourage a greater flow of traffic across the bridge, it would make a singular contribution to the renewal of our public life.

The power of the church to play a public role is illustrated by the experience of the black church in America. Much of the strength blacks have found to engage a society of strangers, an alien and hostile culture, has come from their grounding in the church. The roots of black power are not to be found in a political ideology, but in the opportunity the church has provided for people to gather, to sense and celebrate their solidarity. I once asked a politically active black minister in Washington, D.C. to name the primary task in his ministry. I suppose I expected him to say something about political organizing, protest, and the like. Instead, he said, "To provide my people with a rich social life." I asked, "Do you mean parties and pot-lucks and socials and things like that?" thinking his answer sounded a bit frivolous. "Of course," he said, "things like that give my people the strength to struggle in public."

Of course, the challenge before us is even greater. We need to empower a public of more than one race or ethnic stock or economic status, a public which bridges all these gaps and embraces all the people. But in this task we have much to learn from the history of the black church. We need especially to understand that the "social life" which my minister friend was so intent on nurturing took place within a context of shared stories and symbols and was thus transformed from mere gathering into a celebration of common bonds and mutual loyalties. Within that context, a pot-luck supper means more than getting something to eat and seeing your friends (although it does, and must, mean that). It also means "breaking bread together" with all the spiritual significance those words imply.

The churches of this country still possess the potential for the greatest power of all: the power to infuse life with meaning, or to articulate the meaning with which life is already ripe. Part of that meaning is found in overcoming the loneliness of modern life by discovering and celebrating our common bond. As the church finds words and ways to do that, it will help revitalize our public realm.

5

This book is written in the context of a decade of cultural criticism. In a steady stream of well-known books and articles critics have assailed Americans for taking a perversely inward turn, a turn away from relatedness and responsibility toward untempered self-absorption and self-concern. Though the critique has often been overdrawn, it has been largely on target: there is ample evidence that private preoccupations have overwhelmed our sense of public possibilities during the decade just past. Christians and the church have not been exempt from the critique. Though the "human potential" movement may have led the way toward self-obsession, various versions of the "new spirituality" quickly joined the fad and endowed it with a certain religious respectability.

Some of this criticism has had a salutary effect, creating at least the kind of embarrassment one feels when caught admiring one's face in a mirror. Some of it has encouraged us to recall our relatedness to other people's lives. But the critique has lacked two vital elements. The first is a constructive effort to define, identify, and locate the public life itself. It is easy enough to criticize privatism and self-interest. But where should people go, and what should they do, when they want to take part in public process? Philosophers have written about the public for centuries, but they have not drawn roadmaps or written instruction manuals. Most of what they have said is of little use to a citizen looking for "something public" to do on a Saturday morning. Even if we had some practical suggestions in hand, and the will to use them, our society is deficient in the facilities and opportunities for the interaction of strangers on which public life depends. We need to do more than berate and bemoan our privatism. We need to help each other discover and create occasions for public experience.

Second, this recent body of cultural criticism has been overly cynical about the values of private life itself—I mean the life involving family, friends, self, and the inward journey. Clearly, there are self-contained and selfish ways of living with family and friends, and there are paths of inward journey which lead not outward to community but dead-end in self-worship. But there are other paths of private living and inward travelling which bring us into a deep sense of relatedness with the world. An authentic family life can be lived with public needs in mind; an authentic life of meditation or prayer will lead us time and again to our unity with others in God.

Indeed, the outward life of our time is often so frantic and fragmenting that it does not readily support the presumption of human unity. And the secularization of our society means that the public realm has been stripped of those symbols which might remind us of our God-given relatedness to one another. In the face of these outer discouragements, more and more of us may have to find the private means, the inward ways, of touching those deep places in which we know ourselves to be one with all humanity. Private experience, far from being the enemy of public life, may be the place in which we rediscover our commonality—providing we find the means of taking that discovery back into the public realm.

These two gaps in the critique of "the new narcissism"—its failure to define the public realm, and its failure to give private life its due—are closely related. The private *has* grown out of proportion in our society, and the inward journey *has* been perverted into narcissism, partly *because* we have failed to identify their public counterweight. We need to see that in a healthy society the private and the public are not mutually exclusive, not in competition with each other. They are, instead, two halves of a whole, two poles of a paradox. They work together dialectically, helping to create and nurture one another.

For instance, the individual who plays an active public role needs a nurturing private life. Public life alone has too much centrifugal force; it spins us away from our center and can cause personal fragmentation. It needs to be balanced by the centripetal spin of inward experience which brings us back to the center from which wholeness comes (a wholeness which is not ours alone, but which always embraces others). Conversely, problems we regard as strictly private almost always have important public dimensions in their solutions. Indeed, the very health of the private realm depends on the health of the public sphere. The public is the human environment in which the private exists; if the environment is polluted, then private life will suffer. When people do not care about the common life, when we inch from "benign neglect" toward the war of all against all, there is no way private life can offer security for the individual against anything from crime to the erosion of interpersonal commitments. The excessive privatism of our time is only a misguided effort to preserve values which are threatened by the collapse of our public life.

The public and private are interdependent. When their balance is off, when the dynamic tension between them fails, both will suffer. In our time, public life has withered and private life has become anxious and obsessive. If we could rediscover and recreate the public realm, it would not only be a victory for the public, but would bring new health to private life as well.

Doing so would also bring new health to the church and its relations with society. Recently—perhaps in reaction to a period of private spirituality—certain groups of Christians have moved with strength into the political realm. Their motive is simple: to gain political power. Sometimes their goals seem simple as well: to use that power to impose their own version of Christian virtue on the nation and the world. Such a mission is filled with obvious political dangers in a pluralistic society. It is filled with spiritual dangers as well, the dangers of arrogance and intolerance, of identifying God's will with the self-interest of a small but aggressive community, or even the nation as a whole. If Christians could rediscover and recreate the public realm, as distinct from politics, we could begin to build a community which would hold government accountable to the needs and wishes of all the people.

6

If Christians are to play a role in the renewal of public life, we must undertake several critical tasks, around which the rest of this book is organized.

First, we need to study the nature of the public life and the factors that nurture it. Since our subject is crusted over by centuries of philosophical abstraction and narrow common usage, we need to develop a fresh and vital sense of the public and its life. A concept can serve as a map, but if we get the concept wrong, the map will be more hindrance than help. With a map of public life which reveals roads obscured by conventional definitions, our journey will be easier and more promising.

Second, we need to understand how public life relates to the spiritual core of Christian faith. I do not expect the church to think about or act upon anything which does not flow from its heart—from its desire to seek and celebrate God. I shall try to show how the public life is not incidental to the church's agenda, not an option for Christians who feel so called, but central to our life in the Spirit.

Third, we need to see how public life relates to the other great arenas of human experience—notably, the private and the political. Here, again, my intent is to demonstrate how public life is vital to a whole range of human concerns, from the sanctity of the individual to the processes of big government.

Fourth, we need to ask and answer the question, "What can the church do?" I shall try to do that on three levels. (1) The church can preach and teach a public theology, especially a theology which revolves around two major problems in public life, the problem of scarcity and the problem of conflict. (2) The church can practice the public life within the congregation itself, giving people the confidence and competence to "go public" in larger ways. (3) The church can reach outside its own walls to help create the "public space" in which people can experience themselves as members of one another.

Finally, we need to seek and find the grounds of Christian hope in the midst of our public crisis. Those grounds are to be found in God's promise of reconciliation and God's faithfulness to that promise. We will touch that ground and root ourselves in it through prayer and contemplation—not as an isolated individual act, but as directed and disciplined within the community of faith. Just as private and public life are halves of a larger whole, so private prayer and public worship are meant to be as one.

In all these ways the church can help renew that vision without which the people perish.

2

The Public Life
Its Nature and Nurture

1

Fifty years ago, John Dewey wrote that ". . . the outstanding problem of the Public is the discovery and identification of itself. . . ."[1] As those words suggest, our public life is not dead but invisible. There will always be a public, as long as there are people in societies. The public is all around us all the time, and each of us is always a part of it. But we lack awareness of that fact, appreciation of that opportunity, understanding of the need for conscious public participation. So public life, which could be a force for unity, and a stimulating dimension of individual experience, lies fallow—untapped potential in a society which concentrates its resources on cultivating private experience.

If we are to discover our life as a public and bring it into daily awareness, we must have a working concept of public life—a concept which enables us to see the public where it exists and to rebuild it where it has collapsed. Our ability to see what is around us, or what might be there, depends on the concepts we carry in our heads. If we did not have a concept for "stars" we could not see them for what they are, no matter how numerous and visible the stars might be. Our concepts also limit our ability to act. When astronomical concepts put the earth at the center of the universe, no program of space exploration would have been possible, even if the technology had existed. Our concept of public life has become so empty or narrow or deformed that we are unable to see the public accurately, to act in public creatively. My hope in this chapter is to develop an image of the public which will bring new breadth and vitality to our sense of what that life is and might become.

2

At bottom, the word "public" means all of the people in a society, without distinction or qualification. A public school is a place from which no child is barred, a place where the common culture of a people can be passed along from one generation to the next. A person in public life is one whose career involves accountability to the people as a whole, who carries a public trust. Even the weaker phrase, a public figure, means a person whose life is visible to all who care to watch it. When information appears in the public press it is available to everyone; a public library collects and stores such information so it will be available to persons yet unborn. And the word is used in similar but less grandiose ways, as in the English "pub" or public house which is a gathering place for the whole community.

These uses of the word remind us of the importance of public life. In public we remember that the world consists of more than self and family and friends. We belong to a human community; we are supported by it and must support it; in this world "no man (or woman) is an island." All of this and more is evoked by the idea of a public in its most general sense.

So it is puzzling that the word has come to have such a narrow meaning in our time. Today, in ordinary usage, public means "of or pertaining to government." We commonly think of the public as the body of voters whose primary function is to go to the polls, elect government officials, decide on a few referenda, and retire until the next election. Or we may speak of a public policy, meaning governmental enactments which are binding on all. When we think of a public school, we think of an institution supported by tax monies which the government collects and allocates. Or when we think of a person in public life, we picture someone whose career is in government.

Why has this word—which should evoke the common bond of a diverse people—taken on such narrow political meaning? I suspect the answer lies in an assumption which pervades the political thought of our society, the assumption that only through the processes of government can a public be created, that only through legislative enactments can the many become one.

The mainstream of our political thought has assumed that the individual, by nature, is primarily motivated by self-interest. If that is true, then a public is possible only as ways are found to correlate and control the vast diversity of self-interests. The task of government is to provide a framework of rules and penalties within which a community can be constructed out of the convergence of self-interests, with those interests which do not fit being deflected or simply denied. In this stream of political theory, the public has been reduced to an arena in which individuals compete for the most they can get with government as the referee.

This image of the public contains far less promise than an authentic public life. The regulatory powers of government, however, necessary, can neither give us a vision of unity nor lead us toward community. Such powers can only provide minimal security, a level of survival without quality. The vision and reality of community come when people have direct experience of each other, experience of mutuality and interdependence unmediated by governmental sanctions and codes. The vision and reality of community come when people have a rich array of opportunities to interact in public, interactions which draw out and encourage the human impulse toward life together.

I do not deny the element of self-interest in society. Nor do I deny the need for institutions of government which limit the extent to which self-interest can be pursued. But this is a minimal vision of what is possible among people. If this is all we can say about the public life, we have traded away our birthright. And if we envision the public as nothing more than a battleground between divergent self-interests, we create a dismal self-fulfilling prophecy. Given this image, it is small wonder that fewer and fewer people venture into public without being (figuratively and literally) well-armed. Small wonder that more and more people retreat from the public arena so conceived into the sanctuary of private life.

We need a larger and more inviting image of public possibilities, an image founded in the fact, to quote Robert Bellah, that "a society could not last a single day if its people were motivated by nothing except the maximization of self-interest."[2] If a people lack the impulse to see themselves as one, and the chance to act out that impulse, then no government, however powerful, can hold them together.

Finally, the only limitation on self-interest is other-interest, the sense that we are members of one another for better and for worse. Other-interest comes, in part, as the result of a healthy public life. If self-interest is the dominant mood of our time, it is not because self-interest is the whole of human nature. Instead, it is partly because we lack a public life in which other-interest can be evoked and nurtured.

Human nature is (to understate the case) complex and contradictory. It contains a wide range of possibilities, from the noblest self-sacrifice to the cruellest self-service, as history reveals. But these diverse tendencies of human nature will be amplified or suppressed according to the structures of encouragement, the channels of expression, available at any given time. If we had no structures for private life (e.g., private dwelling quarters, or the institution of the family) private instincts would tend to fade. And so it is with the desire for public experience.

My argument for public possibilities is based on an assumption which can be stated negatively or positively. Negatively: so long as the primary opportunities of our lives are private, our tendency to deny public relatedness will be amplified. Positively: if people are given opportunities for public experience and expression, the experience itself will evoke their willingness, interest, desire, and ability to be part of the public.

That assumption is backed by some hard data, not least the fascinating study by Richard Titmus on the way various countries collect human blood for medical uses. A voluntary system of blood donation, such as that which exists in England, gives people an opportunity to make a significant gift to the stranger; such a system nurtures the public life. But in countries like the United States, where most blood is sold to commercial establishments, what might be a gift to a stranger becomes a sale to a customer instead. Titmus demonstrates that the supply of blood is far superior, both quantitatively and qualitatively, in countries where the voluntary system predominates than it is where blood may be sold for a price. "In some countries," Titmus writes, "the commercialization of blood is discouraging and downgrading the voluntary principle. Both the sense of community and the expression of altruism are being silenced."[3] But a structured opportunity to give a gift to the stranger encourages the impulse toward the public life.

Of course, there are some people who will always resist the public life no matter how many opportunities are offered, and most of us will find it difficult from time to time. But I believe there is an inclination, a tendency, a gravity in the human heart toward one another. We need to establish the conditions under which that tendency can find expression and gain momentum.

If that tendency does not exist in human nature, then there is nothing we can do to force a public into being. But—as Bellah suggests—the very fact that we have a functioning society means that some sort of public spirit is at work, that some forms of public life exist to evoke and channel that spirit. My question is how to widen and multiply the channels so that more of the spirit can flow.

3

If the public life—as I use the phrase—does not happen simply in the halls of government, and does not result simply in public policy decisions, where does it happen and what are its outcomes? As we answer those questions, we will begin to build a working definition. First, a brief survey of some of the places where public life occurs.

The most likely place is in the public street where strangers in pursuit of private interests meet each other. No word may pass between them, but as they walk by, whether dimly aware or actively curious about each other, a public is being formed. In this encounter of strangers, an important subliminal message is being conveyed: we do not know each other, and we may look strange (even ominous) in each other's eyes, but we occupy the same territory, belong to the same human community, and we need to acknowledge that fact and learn to get along.

City parks, squares, sidewalk cafes, museums, and galleries are also settings for the public life. Here, strangers can pause, spend time in each other's presence, share common interests and pleasures, become somewhat more aware of each other, and perhaps even exchange a few words. When a city is rich in facilities such as these, the public life is more likely to thrive. Unfortunately, in most of our cities, heedless planning has made public space scarce, sacrificing it to more profitable uses.

Rallies, forums, hearings, and debates (including those conducted by means of public media) are settings in which the public interacts and becomes aware of itself. Here, strangers have an opportunity to listen and be heard, to air their differences and conflicts, to influence each other's thinking, and to move toward mutual accommodation.

But the public life is not all conflict and accommodation. It is also stimulation, celebration, and enhancement of life through the interaction of diverse people. This side of public experience is most obvious when a street musician is playing, or at carnivals, festivals, and fairs. Here people are not only entertained, but they entertain each other. Here we learn that our interdependence does not simply pose problems; it is also the source of great joy, the joy we find when we receive each other's gifts and share each other's foibles. The public life is the constant enactment of the human comedy, and when we learn to look for that and see it, life is immeasurably enriched.

The neighborhood is another important setting for the public life (though a setting which has been eroded by the trends of privatization and urbanization). The public as a whole is simply too large, too abstract, for the individual to identify with and respond to. A small world like the neighborhood gives the public a human face, a human scale. As we gain experience in the neighborhood, we increase our ability to identify with the public in its larger and more distant forms. The ability to identify with the world community itself depends on having an outward moving series of concentric public experiences, and the neighborhood is often the vital inner circle.

Voluntary associations are also settings in which strangers come together and receive training in the public life. Here we learn that it is possible for people who are neither family nor friends, people whose lives touch only tangentially, to relate within a framework of common interest, concern, commitment; to share scarce resources and make decisions about them even when disagreement exists; to take collective action even when visions differ. By gaining confidence and competence in voluntary associations (including the church) people are empowered to enter larger spheres of public activity.

4

So the settings in which public life happens are many and diverse. What happens in these places which gives them a common public character? What are the outcomes, the results, the consequences of people living in public, as a public? I want to list and comment on ten characteristic functions of the public life as the next step in opening up a new image of public possibilities. With each point I shall try to show how the public encourages a dimension of human experience which private life alone denies us.

Strangers meet on common ground. This is the first and most basic feature of public life. Our sense of being a public depends on the recognition that our lives are intertwined with those of strangers, that we must live in ways which take strangers into account. In private life we concentrate on developing relationships of intimacy; there are no strangers here. In private life the stranger does not intrude (except illegally), and if we invite the stranger in, it is usually because we want to alter our relationship from that of strangers to friends. But in public we are constantly reminded that the foundation of life together is not the intimacy of friends but the capacity of strangers to share a common territory, common resources, common problems—without ever becoming friends. This is the fundamental truth of public life, a lesson not easily learned in our time when the ideal of intimacy overshadows all other forms of human relatedness. The public life is a place where we learn that there can—and must—be honor among strangers as well as among friends.

Fear of the stranger is faced and dealt with. In private life we need deal only with those who are "like us." Only those who satisfy this standard are ordinarily admitted into our private space. For most of us, the private circle of family and friends is confined to persons of the same race, economic status, and life-experience as our own. In private we are deprived of direct experience of the stranger, and we tend to grow afraid of those who are different, afraid of the hidden threats which "otherness" seems to contain. It is a vicious circle, for this fear of strangers bred by an exclusively private life makes it ever more difficult to enter the public realm. But when we participate regularly in public life, the very experience helps destroy our stereotypes and fantasies of "the stranger." Public interaction brings the stranger down to human scale and makes our perceptions less paranoid, more realistic. In public we learn that underneath all surface differences people share a common humanity, and our image of the stranger-as-demon vaporizes and drifts away.

Scarce resources are shared and abundance is generated. The problem of scarcity is one of the basic challenges and sources of public life. If there were more than enough resources, people might have the luxury of living in affluent isolation from one another (indeed, some of us have seized this luxury through private strategies). But since we live in a world of shortages, a public must form to decide how those scarce resources can be distributed to the optimum benefit of all. This process of "deciding" can be rudimentary and nearly unconscious: a crowd on a city sidewalk is learning to share the scarce resource of sidewalk space. Or it can be more conscious and complex: during a recent drought in California, a strong sense of the public developed as people cut back on excessive water consumption so that the minimum collective need could be met.

A public response to scarcity has the potential of generating new abundance. For example, when fire ravages a barn, and neighbors gather to rebuild it at a fraction of the time and cost it would have taken the owner to do it alone, an abundance is created through group effort. Even when the public simply shares scarcity without generating a real abundance of new goods and services, the simple fact of sharing creates a meaningful sense of abundance, the abundance which comes from knowing we do not stand alone or in constant competition with each other but that mutual aid is available. When we live our lives strictly in private, concerned only with our own consumption, when we hoard and do not share, then we live in continual fear of scarcity and never learn of the riches that a public life can bring.

Conflict occurs and is resolved. When strangers meet and must share scarce resources, they do not always succeed, and abundance is not always generated. So conflict is inevitable in the public realm. There is conflict in private too, of course, but because we are more committed to the people in our private lives, we tend to be more hopeful and more energetic about resolving our differences. We fear conflict in public because we do not know its bounds—perhaps it will become painful, even brutal—and so we withdraw from public participation.

But a healthy public life gives us daily experience with conflict. It teaches us that public conflict is not terminal and gives us the skills to work it through. Again, the process can be simple and subtle: that crowd on the city sidewalk is dealing with potential conflict at every moment, for there is not enough space for each person to move as he or she pleases. But in that crowd we learn to adjust, compromise, correct our course so that conflict is minimized and the movement of the whole becomes possible. The lesson is subliminal, but it prepares us for the more difficult and complex forms of conflict which public life poses. When we live our lives largely in private, conflict becomes a spectre which haunts us and keeps us away from the public sphere.

Life is given color, texture, drama, a festive air. If fear and conflict were the primary features of public life, such a life would hold little appeal for us. Unfortunately, this is precisely the image public life has in our time. We have lost our sense of the gaiety of public experience. But in a healthy public realm, the strangers who meet also entertain each other. They bring variety and the unexpected into each other's lives. They provide each other (often inadvertently) with comic relief from the dailyness of life.

The public is inherently interesting. It contains all the variegation of the human species itself. In private, we are never taken beyond that which is familiar to us, that which—even as it comforts us—binds and bores us. In public we are introduced to that which is foreign and exotic and which stretches our minds. Public life gives us a chance to experience the fascination which is the other side of fear, and the creative ferment which is the other side of conflict. I think not only of those formal occasions when the public comes together to celebrate some great event, such as the Fourth of July; I think even more of those random moments when the mingling of strangers at a theater, or in a park, gives rise to a kind of human electricity, a sense of new possibilities, which only life in public can create.

People are drawn out of themselves. In our time we have forgotten the ancient wisdom that the self will wither if we seek it directly, and will flower only as we lose it in service of others. Here is another function of public life: to help us develop the other-interest which can pull us out of simple self-interest (and which, paradoxically, brings us back to our true selves). In public we see all conditions of men and women. Some will evoke our interest, some our sympathy, some our anger, some our gratitude. Whatever our reactions, public life reminds us that the universe is not egocentric. Through public interaction people see that they belong to a community which is larger than self, and on which self depends—a lesson not so easily learned when we stay within a private realm which can so easily revolve around self-interest and personal ease.

Mutual responsibility becomes evident, and mutual aid possible. In public we learn how intertwined our lives really are. Only in private can the illusion flourish that we are autonomous and alone. We could not walk or drive safely down a public street if we did not recognize our mutuality and make adjustments for it. And a healthy public life offers us the opportunity to learn that lesson on even deeper levels. For instance, our private worlds seldom bring us into contact with the poor, the sick, the broken. In fact, we have put much energy into creating private worlds for each of these "classes" of people so they will not haunt our lives. But in an authentic public life, where we would encounter all conditions, the more able among us might develop a deeper sense of our need and capacity to assist our less able brothers and sisters. Jean Vanier (who himself has established villages where the mentally retarded live side-by-side with persons who are not so handicapped) has said of the rich:

> Once in contact with the poor, they will become taken up by distress; not the distress of a bad conscience which refuses compassionate contact, but the distress of wounded people whom they will have seen and touched. Having seen and touched people in distress, they will begin to love, begin to dispossess themselves of their riches, begin to share.[4]

If Vanier seems overly optimistic about the capacity of public life to open the hearts of the wealthy, we can at least claim this: in a privatized society the debate over our mutual obligations becomes distant and abstract, lacking direct encounter with people in need. (How many of those who argue against welfare have spent even a day living with a welfare family in genuine need?) We will build relations of compassion in our society only as more and more people gain personal knowledge of such needs through the flow of public life.

Opinions become audible and accountable. When we express ourselves in public we are heard by strangers who may dispute our facts or hold different points of view. Conversely, in public we have a chance to respond to what others say, a chance to correct their thinking. Expression in public tempers our opinions by holding them up to scrutiny and criticism. In private there is no check; in private we can say what we please without rebuttal—no matter how erroneous or damaging to others. So the formation of "public opinion" involves more than changing percentage points on a Gallup poll. It involves the process by which members of the public educate themselves and each other. In this process individuals learn that private viewpoints have implications for the common good. In this process a conception of the common good is shaped from the interaction of individual points of view.

Vision is projected and projects are attempted. No significant vision can find full expression within the confines of private life. Sooner or later, if it is to be fulfilled, it must find an outlet in the public realm. It may be an idea, a book, a work of art, a social movement or program. Impulses such as these, however private their origins, seek public expression as a plant seeks light—and for much the same reason: to be nurtured into growth. A story needs to be told and heard before it is a real story. A work of art needs to be seen and enriched by the viewer before it comes to fruition. A social program becomes what it is only as the public joins in. Such projects may not survive public exposure, sometimes for better, sometimes for worse (for the public is not always right). But the power of public life is such that only through its processes can visions born in private become most fully real.

People are empowered and protected against power. It is no accident that totalitarian countries have all but extinguished the public life, except for those staged occasions when a pseudo-public is gathered to jump through the government's hoops. For public life both empowers people to influence the government and protects people against excessive incursions of governmental power. Such empowerment happens in several ways. The public life teaches us about our common interests and difficulties and thus strengthens us against the illusion that we stand alone, an illusion which makes us all too vulnerable to massive central power. The public life gives us opportunities to band together, as in rallies or marches, to demonstrate the size and intensity of our collective sentiment. And as we undertake projects in the public realm, we learn the skills of collective action, skills of leadership and decision-making and creative resolution of conflict. Where no public life exists and citizens remain (or are kept) in private isolation, central government can amass power unchecked—and when enough power has been gathered, the private realm is abolished, too, making government the only actor on the stage.

A healthy public life is vital in the continuing struggle toward freedom and equality for all people. But that movement does not begin with politics, with the formal institutions of government. It begins with the simple opportunities of public interaction: the chance to meet strangers, to deal with fear and conflict, to realize and celebrate our diversity and the unity that lies beneath it.

5

Opportunities for public interaction do not just happen. They depend on the presence of certain facilitating factors. By understanding some of these factors we will both deepen our idea of public life and get clues about practical steps toward the renewal of public experience. I want to explore three such factors here: public space, a public psychology, and a public myth.

There can be no public interaction without physical space which encourages the encounter of strangers. Historically, the primary public space has been found in the marketplace or streets where people come in pursuit of private interest (shopping, work, or simply getting from one place to another) and in the process meet as a public.

The capacity of the streets to encourage a public life is enhanced by a rich mix of private, semiprivate, and public usages within a limited area. For example, public interaction is increased if, within a few square blocks, one finds residences, shops, offices, and a square or park—for these different usages will guarantee a mix of different kinds of people moving through the space in different rhythms all through the day. But if, block after block, one finds only residences, or only places of work, the public life is undermined. In such areas persons of one kind predominate; they tend to move in and out on identical schedules, thus not mixing with each other; and they have no reason to step outside their private homes or work spaces except to travel to some distant and equally segregated office or residential area.

Our present arrangements of space do not enhance the public life, with residence here, shopping there, and employment somewhere else. By segregating these functions we have made public interaction all but impossible in many places. We go to work and disappear inside our office for the day. We go home and disappear inside the house for the night. And when we go shopping, we often go to places which may seem public but, in fact, contain far less public life than the marketplace or streets: I refer to the ubiquitous shopping mall.

The mall appears to be a place of public life and (as I shall try to show later) it has that potential. But the typical shopping mall tends to repress rather than evoke public experience. The strangers one encounters on the city streets are, for the most part, fellow citizens of the local community, and the public life is enhanced by this sense of geographic relatedness. But the mall, as one writer has put it, is a "placeless space." It is not identified with any local community, but strives to create a fantasy environment conducive only to shopping, not to the cultivation of public relatedness:

> . . . if malls have a mind set, a spiritual epicenter, it's not the city, the suburb or rural America, but out *there,* in between, just off the highway. . . . These alien forms, with their magnetic power to attract customers and retailers from everywhere, are rearranging the landscape. The suburban malls found they were creating new traffic patterns, drawing customers from cities and towns and other suburbs as far as 40 to 60 miles away. . . . "Developers learned they could get away with a minimum of relationship to the community and still attract thousands."[5]

Not only is the mall unrelated to the local community; it disrupts the patterns of local life. The regional mall dries up the traditional shopping centers, draining commerce from downtown areas, leaving the public heart of our towns and cities empty and lifeless. In their place, the mall offers a center for commercial, not civic, interaction, devoid of any public purpose.

This is not just a sociological tendency of malls; it has the full status of law. On the public streets, the interaction of strangers always has the potential of flowering into more explicit forms of public life—such as leafletting, soliciting signatures for petitions, soapbox oratory, rallies, marches, and the like. But the mall has put a crimp in these possibilities, for the mall, unlike the streets, is private property and thus not available for public activities—especially if those activities have political overtones. In many places, people who have tried to demonstrate in malls have simply been evicted, and the courts have often upheld the right of mall owners to do so: "The total power of the mall owner, even when civil liberties are involved, has been upheld by the courts. . . . According to the Supreme Court, malls can keep out those who threaten . . . to disturb the fantasy world inside."[6] The mall, rather than offering a crossroad for private and public experience, represents the trend in our society toward an all-embracing private sphere.

Malls have grown in part because we perceive the city streets to be unsafe. So the mall becomes a private answer to a public problem. But the answer is misguided. Instead of seeking public remedies to the causes of urban violence, we expand the sovereignty of private space. This reliance on private space also explains our unwillingness to give up the automobile. For millions of people, the auto is the only safe way in which to pass through dangerous public space; we drive daily through places where we could not dream of walking. We are willing to absorb the expense, the congestion, and the filth caused by the auto (rather than invest seriously in public transportation) because the auto is private, safe, and secure.

The problem of unsafe streets is partly real, partly a figment of overactive imaginations working in a vacuum of public experience. But more important, it is a vicious circle, a self-fulfilling prophecy. When we begin to think of space as unsafe, we withdraw from it, and as we withdraw from it, it becomes unsafe. Space is kept secure not primarily by good lighting or police power but by the presence of a healthy public life. If the space is such that a rich mix of people are using it; if the space is such that people regard it as theirs and care for it; then that space will be as safe as it can be. The public use of public space provides more safety than private strategies will ever afford.

6

A second factor which can help or hinder the life of the public is the psychology or mind-set of the time. Richard Sennett has made an important contribution to our understanding of the public psychology by analyzing the "ideology of intimacy" which dominates our sense of how we should relate to others:

> The reigning belief today is that closeness between persons is a moral good. The reigning aspiration today is to develop individual personality through experiences of closeness and warmth with others. The reigning myth today is that the evils of society can all be understood as the evils of impersonality, alienation, and coldness. The sum of these three is an ideology of intimacy: social relationships of all kinds are real, believable, and authentic the closer they approach the inner psychological concerns of each person. This ideology transmutes political categories into psychological categories. This ideology of intimacy defines the humanitarian spirit of a society without gods; warmth is our god.[7]

Intimacy itself is not a bad thing; that is not the problem. Nor is it the case that intimacy and public life cannot coexist. Intimate private relations can obviously exist alongside the relations of strangers in public, and we sometimes know fleeting but powerful moments of intimacy even with strangers; hence, the oft-noted tendency for people to share their problems with a stranger on the train or plane, a sharing which is possible in part because the two will never seen each other again. Indeed, when I argue that public life is ultimately grounded in an inward, spiritual sense of our relatedness to strangers, I am rooting the public life in a kind of intimacy—the intimacy we have in God.

The problem arises when closeness and warmth become the criteria of all meaningful relations, when we reject and even fear relationships which do not yield to these standards. The problem arises when we impose the norm of intimacy (which applies primarily to private life) upon the public sphere. For within the public realm, where most relations are necessarily distant and impersonal, the demand for closeness and warmth distorts and eventually destroys the potential of public experience.

As Sennett points out, we have imposed the demand for intimacy on our public experience, but in a most ambivalent way. On the one hand, fearing the impersonality of the public realm and wanting to personalize it, we become intrigued with the personalities and private lives of public people. Thus, the success of a political candidate has as much to do with "charisma" as with his or her positions on issues. But the way in which we personalize the public life causes us to fear it even more, for we realize that if we were to enter the public ranks our own personalities and private lives would become subject to scrutiny and criticism. And so we withdraw. We are in a double-bind, wanting to personalize public experience to make it less fearsome, yet simultaneously fearing the consequences of projecting our own personalities onto the public screen.

Historically, Americans have worried about the incursion of public powers into the private realm. But now we can see that there is also a problem when the psychology of private relations is forced upon the public sphere. When intimacy becomes the sole criterion for authentic human relationships, we falsify relations in public; hence, the cult of personality which has so distorted our political process. We must learn to accept and appreciate the fact that public life is fundamentally impersonal. Relations in public are the relations of strangers who do not, and need not, know each other in depth. And such relations have real virtue. The public life involves those qualities of distance and disinterest which allow us to receive from another without assuming a personal obligation, to give to another without having to make a total commitment. In fact, the public life allows us to view and listen to each other, to be edified and entertained, without forming a personal relationship of any sort. To receive full benefit from public life, one must realize that impersonal relations have a validity of their own.

All of this is denied by the ideology of intimacy which sees virtue only in closeness and warmth and finds distant relations either meaningless or ominous. But a moment's reflection will reveal the positive place of impersonality in our lives. We sometimes need relationships which allow distance, or we end up feeling smothered and cramped. We need relationships which do not ask us to reveal the whole self, or we risk having no independent self at all. We need involvements which do not lay total claim on our lives, or there will be no room for the unique and unexpected to rise up in us. In an impersonal relationship we are sometimes seen (and see ourselves) more clearly than in an intimate one, and are thus given special opportunities to grow. In all of these respects, the company of strangers can be an enriching complement to the relations of family and friends.

Some readers may be unconvinced by the thesis that we impose intimate norms on public life, pointing to the fact that millions of us engage daily in impersonal relations with sales clerks, news vendors, railroad conductors—without either feeling fear or seeking closeness. But these relations are carefully governed by role definitions: one person is a customer who seeks to have a need met, while the other is a dispenser who controls the goods or services desired. What we fear, and seek either to avoid or personalize, are the undefined and uncontrolled relations of strangers in public. Imagine, for example, that you are walking through a park and see a crowd gathering around a particular spot. One's first thought is usually an ominous one: either a fight has started or an accident has happened. Drawing close for benign purposes is something only intimates do, and when it happens among people passing through a park, there must be trouble afoot. It is hard for us to imagine that such a gathering of persons in a public place might be for purposes that are constructive or creative—a debate, for example, or enjoyment of a street musician, or spontaneous celebration of some happy piece of news.

We need to cultivate a new imagination, a new psychology. If we can affirm the positive value of the relation of strangers, and let that image lead us into new patterns of behavior, we can help renew the public's life.

7

A third factor which makes public life possible is the structure of myth and symbol—indeed, the theology—which defines us as a public to begin with. By "myth," of course, I do not mean a fairy tale or lie. I mean a way of looking at the world which helps explain that world and one's place in it, which tells us what is important and meaningful out of all of life's options.

Sennett argues that "warmth is our god." On one level, he is right; we revere relations of warmth as the only meaningful kind. But Sennett misses our inner ambivalence, our unconscious knowledge that this is a god which will always fail us, our instinctive sense that close and warm relations are hard to find and even harder to sustain. So we have a back-up theology which worships no relationship at all, but only the career of the autonomous self. In this myth, the hero is the self-seeking ego who cuts loose from the community to become what he or she wishes to become, on his or her own terms, with no reference to corporate membership or public need. It is the myth of Narcissus whose only object of contemplation was his own image in a pool. Clearly, there can be no public life when the eyes we look into are not those of other persons, but only our own, reflected in a mirror.

It has not always been so, even in this American society so long devoted to the development of the individual. Our history is full of powerful symbols of public life, symbols which allowed people to understand themselves as a public and which animated them to play a public role. The founders of this society understood themselves not as a collection of individuals but as a community, a "New Israel," a "Chosen People," who had set off on an "Exodus" to establish themselves in a "New Jerusalem" or "New Canaan." England was "Egypt," King James I was the "Pharoah," and the Atlantic Ocean was the "Red Sea." The colonists—standing in this ancient tradition—believed that they, like the first Israel, had been selected by God for a special mission in history, to be a "city set upon a hill" for the example and inspiration of others. The community they were to establish in "the promised land" had a special messianic character: it was ignited by God to give light to a world lost in the dark.

At the core of this myth, this complex of symbols, so influential in the colonial period of our society, is a master symbol, a controlling metaphor, which holds all the rest together. This is the idea of "covenant." Those who settled this country saw themselves bonded to each other in community because of their bond or covenant with God. They believed that if they were faithful to God, God would hold them together in community. Without denying that economic and political factors played an important role in the formation of colonial America, I claim only that in those early days, religion functioned exactly as the etymology of the word suggests—to bind a people together.

Nor can we ignore the fact that the colonists operated with a tragically exclusive definition of "the people." As with the Greek conception of "public," the colonial understanding of covenant failed to create a society of equity for all. Native Americans, the original inhabitants of the land and, later, blacks brought over as slaves, were regarded as beyond the pale. But these exclusions are not inherent in the idea of covenant itself. As I shall argue later in more detail, the colonists perverted the covenant idea, using it to create a community of privilege rather than compassion and service. The problem is not in the biblical idea of covenant but in the self-serving human sense of what "chosenness" means.

As we look back on our early history and then glance again at our own time, it is tempting to write off this formative American myth as an anachronism, a relic, a fossil covered over by decades of secularism and rationalism. But that would be a mistake. For as we trace American history after the colonial era, it becomes clear that the covenant symbol continues to be central in American life, even though it takes various disguises, changing shapes and forms.

The secularization of public language occurred early in American history, even as early as the Declaration of Independence. Here, though God is mentioned, the language begins to "cool" in comparison with the fervent usages of the Massachusetts Bay Colony and the First Great Awakening. The Declaration speaks of "the Laws of Nature and Nature's God," of the "Creator," the "Supreme Judge," and of "Divine Providence"—all references more characteristic of a sophisticated deism than of passionate biblical faith. And as we move on to the Constitution of the United States, we find no explicit reference to God or to God's covenant with the people. Indeed, the only reference to religion is found in the so-called "wall of separation" clause, leading some observers to claim that the mentality of its writers was essentially secular, devoid of religious imagination.

But neither the Declaration nor the Constitution is a rejection of the history and religious imagery which preceded it. Instead both documents are manifestations of that history, and neither document is conceivable without the history from which it emerges. Though the Constitution does not mention "covenant," it is itself a covenant which was drafted and ratified within an ethos of covenant thought-patterns which had been building for years. The covenant imagery "disappeared" in the Constitution only in the sense that it was taken for granted.

I stress this point because it is a mistake to imagine that religious symbolism is no longer capable of animating American public life. Of course, there are problems of translation; we no longer speak as the Puritans did. But the idea of covenant continues to undergird the American mind-set, no matter how far it has sunk into the unconscious realm. In fact, as psychologists tell us, that which is unconscious may have a more powerful impact on our behavior than that which is at the front of our minds. The covenant symbol is implicit, for example, in those voluntary associations still so central to American life—those little covenant groups where people join in a common commitment which, however dimly it may reflect its origins, still links us to our covenantal past. By seeing the presence of the covenant symbol in our collective unconscious, and by finding new ways to articulate it and bring it to awareness, the church could help revive the withering public myth.

Persons concerned to revive the religious grounds of public life often look with nostalgia at times when religious symbols and meanings were prominent in America's public sphere. But the process of secularization has meant driving those symbols from the public realm into the confines of private life. Perhaps, instead of bemoaning this fact, we can capitalize upon it. Perhaps the revival of America's public life will be aided most by those who learn to go deeply within, those who (as Thomas Merton did) touch the heart of God within themselves, that heart in which they are related to all other selves. Perhaps it is from such inner journeying that some will emerge with new symbols and images which can be shared in public to help create the public. The inward turn of America's religious life is fatal to the public only if it does not go far enough. The inward search, if it goes deep, will touch the One who makes us one, a source of new power for the revival of public life.

Such a revival is not without precedent in our land. In the late eighteenth and early nineteenth centuries, the power of religious symbolism to animate American life was on the wane. Deism, disestablishment, and the dispersions of the westward trek were among the factors threatening the power of the church to inform our public life. But it was in that context that the country was swept by the Second Great Awakening, an inward awakening of the outward covenant which America needed to expand and diversify within a framework of national unity.

If there is hope for our future, it is not to be found in calculations predicated on the past. I mention the Second Awakening only as a reminder that God has acted to bring us together when there was felt need among the people and openness to new leadings. Perhaps the greatest contribution the church can make to the renewal of our public life is to help people feel the need to revive our sense of commonality, and cultivate the openness of heart which will allow God to raise up a new symbol of that reality in our midst.

Public space, public psychology, and public myth: these are not the only factors which make public life possible, but they are three of the most important. They are also three areas in which I believe the church can have some special impact, so I devote the second half of this book to showing how the church can preach a public theology, practice a public psychology, and create public space. But before moving to those practical suggestions, I want to deepen our understanding of the church's relation to public life, first by showing how the public is a unique and indispensable setting for our own spiritual growth.

3

A Spirituality of Public Life
The Stranger as Spiritual Guide

1

If Christians are to give the public the attention it deserves, we must see that public life is not merely an option for those who feel called to it. Nor is concern for public life ultimately justified by the fact that only there can Christians act out their belief in the unity of all people. Deeper still, the public life is an arena of spiritual experience, a setting in which God speaks to us and forms our hearts with words we cannot hear in the private realm. If we deprive ourselves of public experience, we deny ourselves a unique and compelling form of spiritual growth, a unique and compelling sort of communication with God. Though I believe—and will argue later—that the public life is vital because of its personal and political implications, the heart of my case for the public involvement of Christians lies here: without public experience we cannot experience the fullness of God's word for our lives.

2

The key figure in public life is the stranger. The stranger is also a central figure in biblical stories of faith, and for good reason. The religious quest, the spiritual pilgrimage, is always taking us into new lands where we are strange to others and they are strange to us. Faith is a venture into the unknown, into the realms of mystery, away from the safe and comfortable and secure. When we remain in the security of familiar surroundings, we have no need of faith. The very idea of faith suggests a movement away from our earthly securities into the distant, the unsettling, the strange.

Even if we stay at home, even if we are not on a conscious pilgrimage, the stranger who comes into our lives may well be a pilgrim bearing news. Through the stranger we may have something of the unsettling Spirit brought into our domesticated lives. As Thomas Merton once wrote, ". . . no man knows that the stranger he meets . . . is not already an invisible member of Christ and perhaps one who has some providential or prophetic message to utter."[1] When we meet the stranger, we are engaged in public life, and through such engagement, according to Scripture, gifts of the Spirit will be brought into our lives.

In the letter to the Hebrews, the writer advises, "Let brotherly love continue. Do not neglect to show hospitality to strangers, for thereby some have entertained angels unawares" (13:1–2). The reference is to a story told in the eighteenth chapter of Genesis where strangers appear to Abraham and Sarah at their tent in Hebron and are welcomed, offered refreshment and rest. The strangers then announce that Sarah, who is well past childbearing age, shall give birth to a son, who is Isaac, the second patriarch of the Hebrew people. As the story unfolds, it becomes clear that these visitors are angels of the Lord, messengers sent to convey and fulfill God's promise to Abraham—the promise that Abraham will be given many descendants, and that they will be given the land. Had Abraham and Sarah not been willing to meet the strangers openly and in good faith, they might have blocked the promise from being fulfilled.

This theme is struck again in the twenty-fourth chapter of the gospel according to Luke. Here, the story is set just after Jesus' crucifixion. The women go to the tomb and find it empty; they report this fact (along with the prophecy that Jesus would be resurrected) to the apostles, who react with skepticism: "these words seemed to them an idle tale, and they did not believe them" (24:11). Later that day two of the apostles are walking along the road when they encounter a stranger. The stranger asks them why they seem downcast, and the apostles tell them of Jesus' death and of their doubt that he has been truly resurrected. The stranger says,

> "O foolish men, and slow of heart to believe all that the prophets have spoken!" . . . And beginning with Moses and all the prophets, he interpreted to them in all the scriptures the things concerning himself.
> So they drew near to the village to which they were going. He appeared to be going further, but they constrained him, saying, "Stay with us, for it is toward evening and the day is now far spent." So he went in to stay with them. When he was at table with them, he took the bread and blessed, and broke it, and gave it to them. And their eyes were opened and they recognized him . . . he was known to them in the breaking of bread. (24:25, 27, 28–31, 35)

That stranger, of course, was the risen Christ. Had the apostles failed to extend hospitality to the stranger, they might not have learned that the promise of resurrection had been fulfilled.

In both of these stories the stranger is a bearer of truth which might not otherwise have been received. Both stories tell us that our everyday perceptions and assumptions must be shaken by the intrusion of strangeness if we are to hear God's word. The stories use extreme examples of unexpected truth: an aged woman bearing a child, a dead man coming back to life. But even with lesser truths we often need the stranger's line of vision to help us see straight. For example, each of us has potentials and limitations which become invisible to us and those near us; we "cannot see the forest for the trees." But when the stranger comes along and looks at us afresh, without bias or preconception, those qualities may quickly become apparent. People who serve as consultants to organizations know how often a slight change in angle of vision can open up a new truth. A group may be blocked by a simple problem which the outsider can see and remedy, a problem which the group had taken as a given simply because they had lived with it so long.

This function of the stranger in our lives is grounded in a simple fact: truth is a very large matter, and requires various angles of vision to be seen in the round. It is not that our view is always wrong and the stranger's always right, but simply that the stranger's view is different, giving us an opportunity to look anew upon familiar things.

The role of the stranger in our lives is vital in the context of Christian faith, for the God of faith is one who continually speaks truth afresh, who continually makes all things new. God persistently challenges conventional truth and regularly upsets the world's way of looking at things. It is no accident that this God is so often represented by the stranger, for the truth that God speaks in our lives is very strange indeed. Where the world sees impossibility, God sees potential. Where the world sees comfort, God sees idolatry. Where the world sees insecurity, God sees occasions for faith. Where the world sees death, God proclaims life. God uses the stranger to shake us from our conventional points of view, to remove the scales of worldly assumptions from our eyes. God *is* a stranger to us, and it is at the risk of missing God's truth that we domesticate God, reduce God to the role of familiar friend.

In the two stories I have cited there is a particular kind of truth which the stranger comes to announce—the truth that God keeps the promises God makes. In both of these stories the stranger is a person of promise, and in both stories two promises are being kept. One is the promise of covenant, the promise that God will be faithful to people of faith. The strangers at Hebron brought word of the continuation of Abraham's lineage and land. The stranger who appeared to the apostles brought living word of the resurrection, God's sign of a new covenant. In the covenant we find the religious core of public life, a life of unity among all who know themselves to be children of God. In receiving the stranger, we perform an act of faith which opens the covenant to us.

The second promise kept in both these tales is the promise of newness, the promise that God will continually move among and within us, bringing fresh vitalities and new possibilities to life—if we have eyes to see and ears to hear, if we are capable of receiving the stranger. The new is always strange to us, so it is no accident that the stranger fulfills the promise of newness in our lives.

One of the great spiritual maladies of our time is boredom, the opposite of newness, a boredom bred of the monotony of routine in a bureaucratic, technological society. And as we retreat further and further into private life our boredom deepens. The private is the realm of the familiar, and though the familiar brings us comfort, too much comfort can anesthetize our spirits. The public, however, is the realm of the novel and the strange, and one of the great rewards of being in public is the banishment of boredom from our lives. Though that which is novel and strange can generate anxiety and fear, experience in public can help us move beyond these negative feelings (as we discover how winsome and intriguing the stranger often is) toward a receptiveness to the new. As we move beyond fear we will be able to receive the gift the stranger offers, the fulfillment of God's promise of new life.

Though boredom may seem to be a strictly personal, private problem, it is finally a public concern. Boredom breeds violence as people strike out to find something that will quicken the pulse, something which will make them feel alive again. Violence against the stranger—so common in our day—comes partly from our fear of all things strange. But it comes, too, from our deep need to escape the passivity of a consumption-oriented, spectator society; it comes from our need to escape the self-defined private realm, to push against some "otherness" and get a response. A healthy public life allows us to escape boredom without recourse to violence, a chance to be real persons in a world of other persons, acting and reacting, initiating and responding. But only as we enter and participate in the public life will the stranger be able to deliver this gift, the gift of new life which God has promised.

3

The letter to the Hebrews gives us further insight into this relation between the stranger and God's promise of new life. Here, the writer defines faith as "the assurance of things hoped for, the conviction of things not seen" (11:1). Then he cites those forerunners of Jesus who possessed such faith and thus served as channels for God to bring the future into being: Abel, Enoch, Noah, Abraham, Sarah. About them the writer says,

These all died in faith, not having received what was promised, but having seen it and greeted it from afar, and having acknowledged that they were strangers and exiles on the earth. For people who speak thus make it clear that they are seeking a homeland. If they had been thinking of that land from which they had gone out, they would have had opportunity to return. But as it is, they desire a better country, that is, a heavenly one. Therefore God is not ashamed to be called their God, for he has prepared for them a city. (11:13–16).

This is an important passage for our time, in part because it reminds us that God's promises sometimes take long years to work themselves out, that to stand in faith is to stand in patient trust that those promises will someday be fulfilled. But the passage speaks to us with special force because we ourselves feel like strangers and exiles in our own land.

We are not desert nomads like the early Hebrew people, but neither is our experience so far removed from theirs: one-third of all Americans change their place of residence in any given year. In some ways our situation is more difficult than the life of the wandering Jews. Their whole community moved as one, while we move individually, apart from the friends and relatives who are the fabric of our lives.

Even if we don't change our own physical location, the society around us changes more rapidly than we can accommodate or understand. Perhaps it is the pace of modern change, more than anything else, which makes us feel like "exiles on the earth." It is not only technological change which makes us nervous, with machines taking over more and more human functions. It is not simply ecological change, with green space diminishing while concrete and steel spread. No, we are most fundamentally threatened by changing human relationships. We are comfortable in neighborhoods populated by people of similar social background, but when strangers move in we feel somehow not at home. We want our children to go to school with others of their same race and status, and feel exiled when the law requires the schools to become microcosms of the large society. We feel at home when we can stay within an enclave, surrounded and protected by people "of our own kind"; we feel exiled when exposed to the larger society with all its pluralism and variety. We yearn, some of us, for an earlier time when the enclaves were more secure, when people stayed "in their place," when human relations were more predictable and comforting.

For many Americans, there is a golden age of memory (however illusory) when life was simple, communities more homogeneous, when the lines between groups were clear and strangers did not have to mix. This golden age is analogous to the "land" mentioned in the passage from Hebrews, the land abandoned when the wandering Israelites went into exile. This is the old country, the memory of a safe and secure past, a symbol of the constant temptation to abandon the loneliness of the quest and return to the familiar and the known.

The writer of the letter to the Hebrews says that Israel "would have had the opportunity to return" to this land if they had wished. For us, that is not the case. Our golden age of memory is partly fiction to begin with, and even if it were not, it could never be reconstructed. And I wonder if it would have been possible for the Hebrews to return? Through God's movement in history they had been called into wandering and exile. God had taken them apart from the land of their origins and set them to searching the earth for a new and better land: to go home would surely have involved an intolerable sense of failure, of possibilities untapped.

Could we not see our own situation in this same light? Is it not possible that the social upheavals of our day—our own sense of being exiles on earth—are God's way of calling us into a new future, away from the divisions of the past toward a holy city? Surely this is the opportunity hidden in the conflict of the races, in the crisis of the rich and the poor: the opportunity to see the need for and the signs of a "better country." Biblical faith always requires that we discern God's movement not only in times past but in our own, and the letter to the Hebrews gives us clues about what our own feelings of exile might mean.

If we seek to return to the past, the writer is telling us, it is a sign that we lack faith, whether that past is fantasy or fact. If we seek to return to the golden age of memory where we feel safe and at home, we reveal our distrust of the God who calls us forward. In fact, the writer suggests, the desire to feel at home is a sign of apostasy toward the God who always beckons us toward new lands, new life, and into all the risks of sojourning on earth. But if we are willing to live like "strangers and exiles" that is a sign we are living in faith.

What a curious inversion—taking feelings of estrangement which we normally try to get rid of and calling them positive signs of vocation instead! By this logic, the need to feel at home turns out to be idolatry, for it involves finding our security in position and place rather than in dependence upon God. If we live in God, we will find ourselves on pilgrimage; we will be taken to alien places where we are strangers and estranged. Only when we acknowledge that "you can't go home again" will be on the road to faith.

People who can speak of themselves as strangers and exiles, says the writer of Hebrews, "make it clear that they are seeking a homeland, . . . they desire a better country, that is, a heavenly one." That seeking and that desire lie behind all our contempory uprootedness, I think. Inside each of us there is the knowledge, however dim, that we cannot go back, that the past must not be allowed to strangle the future. The white suburbanites who have fled "changing neighborhoods" once or twice and see change occurring again know, deep inside, that there is nowhere left to run, that they must somehow learn to live with diversity. None of us truly wants the tension, the sense of precariousness which comes with trying to protect some narrow image of what our social life should be. It is simply too stressful to live in this kind of world always fearing, always avoiding, always resisting the strangeness around us. Instead of letting our feelings of exile and estrangement push us backward into illusions of security, we must allow those feelings to call us forward in a quest for a better land. As we do so, God will give us the faith and strength to make the difficult journey.

"Therefore God is not ashamed to be called their God, for he has prepared for them a city." Here is the ultimate biblical rationale for suffering the loneliness of exile. God has promised us a city where our exile will end, where we will be truly at home. If we are willing to live by that promise, to wander as strangers in strange lands in search of that city, God will call us God's people,

God's own. If we accept God's promise and live our lives seeking its fulfillment, God will not be ashamed to be called our God. Then we will receive the promise of covenant in which God makes all strangers as one.

So once again, the stranger becomes the person of promise. The stranger who comes to us may have some word of the search for God's city; when we come as a stranger to others, we may have some word for them. Indeed, the holy city arises in the very process of strangers coming together and bringing word of life to each other. For this is a city in which strangers mingle unafraid, able to deliver their gifts and bring each other new life. This is a city in which the public life is fulfilled.

4

I have been speaking of the stranger in the most general sense, the sense in which we are all strangers to one another outside the circle of family and friends. But in Jesus' ministry the stranger has a much more specific indentity: he or she is one of those who suffer most, who is among the lowliest and most outcast of society. In this view, the stranger is not simply an individual, but one who represents an entire class of people who are pressed to the bottom layer of our world. This special kind of stranger demands our attention, because this stranger is central both to Christian understanding and to the problem of the public life.

In Matthew's gospel, chapter 25, Jesus describes the "last judgment," that point when God will separate the righteous from the unrighteous, the sheep from the goats. And by what standard will we be judged? Not by the minor moralities which some Christians cling to, but according to whether we fed the hungry, gave drink to the thirsty, clothed the naked, visited the sick and imprisoned, and *welcomed the stranger.* And the Lord will say to the people, "Truly . . . as you did it to one of the least of these my brethren, you did it unto me" (25:40).

What the stranger has in common with the criminal, the sick, the hungry and ill-clothed people of our land is that all of these are outcasts, ignored by the comfortable and well-to-do. All of these are objects of fear, a fear which runs so deep we have invented entire institutions to keep such folk "out of sight, out of mind." In fact, all of these people are strangers. It is their strangeness which puts us off; we are estranged from all of them.

Why does Jesus call our attention to the stranger? Deeper still, why does he hinge our salvation on the extent to which we have welcomed and served the stranger in our midst? On the face of it, the answer seems simple and direct: these are people in need, and we will be judged by our willingness to share our abundance with those who have little or nothing. Surely that is true. But it is also a partial and dangerous view of our relation to the stranger, dangerous because it leads us into *noblesse oblige,* into the self-righteousness which comes from feeling we have "done good" for someone, into paternalism and subtle oppression of those who are "lower" than we.

We gain a deeper understanding of our relation to the stranger when we remember that Jesus did not merely point to, but identified himself with the sick, the prisoner, the stranger: "Truly . . . as you did it to one of the least of these my brethren, you did it unto me." If we can take that statement seriously, we can see how central is the stranger to the Christian conception of life. The stranger is not simply one who needs us. We need the stranger. We need the stranger if we are to know Christ and serve God, in truth and in love. For it is only by knowing the truth and by serving in love that we ourselves will be set free.

Neither truth nor love tends to flow freely when we are comfortably in the middle of society, successful in society's terms, profiting from the way things are arranged. Certain crucial truths about our lives are more easily seen when we are on the edge, at the margin, when we are poor or sick or hungry or in prison—and these truths can break the heart open to compassion. When we live on the edge, or take the view of those who do, we can more clearly see our world and what the Lord requires. I am reminded of John Howard Griffin, a white man who dyed his skin black and travelled in the South. By putting himself in the place of the stranger, he was able to see things about America's racism which no white man could ever see—as witness his powerful book *Black Like Me.*

The viewpoint of the stranger not only affords a fuller look at the outer world; it also gives us a deeper look at ourselves. For the stranger represents possibilities in our own lives which we want to avoid facing. We do not want to look at the sick and the dying because we know that someday we will become sick and die. We do not want to look at the hungry and naked and homeless because we fear falling into those calamities ourselves. We do not want to confront the prisoner because we know our own crimes. We avoid the stranger because he or she reminds us of our precarious place on earth, reminds us that we ourselves are strangers to others.

And we are strangers to ourselves as well. To be comfortable with the external stranger we must be comfortable with the stranger within. But we are not. There are parts of each of us which are poverty-stricken, homeless, hungry for nurture of one kind or another. But instead of embracing these inward needs and seeing that they are fed, we deny them, pretending that we have no needs at all. Wanting to project an image of wholeness and success, we flee from those parts of ourselves that feel failed and broken. To deal with the strangers of whom Jesus speaks is simply too painful; they remind us of parts of ourselves we want desperately to forget.

So long as we remain caught in the cycle of fright and flight, no healing will come, either in the outer world or in the inner. By turning away from "the least of these" we reinforce our fear that someday we will find ourselves in their place—and that others will turn away from us. For our fear is not only that we will become hungry or sick, but that we do not live in a society where compassion and help are available. The stranger threatens because he or she evokes the spectre of aloneness in a world whose bonds of mutual concern seem to deteriorate daily. We retreat from the stranger because we want to avoid that awful knowledge of our world—and of our place in it. And as we do so, we create another self-fulfilling prophecy: as we avoid the stranger to avoid being reminded of our own isolation, we create a world in which our isolation deepens.

When Jesus identifies with the outcast and oppressed, he suffers with them, and his suffering brings redemption. When he invites us into compassion for the poor, he invites us into redemption as well. The poor and the hungry and the sick and the stranger—without and within—bring us the Christ; they bring us the opportunity to receive the gift of compassion in our lives and to be saved ("made whole") by sharing that gift with others. The stranger offers us the chance to come out of ourselves and thus to find ourselves. By ministering to the sick and the hungry and the imprisoned we do ourselves more good than we do them; and when we turn our back on "the least of these," we turn our back on God and on our own true selves.

So the public realm where strangers meet is finally a proving ground for faith. In every encounter with every stranger we are given the chance to meet the living Christ. No matter how often we turn that chance down, it is offered again and again and again.

5

In Christian tradition, there is one word above all others which suggests the quality we should seek in meeting with strangers. It is the word "hospitality." I want to explore that word because it focuses on our relation to the stranger, and on a practice which bridges the private and the public realms.

Unfortunately, we have lost the ancient sense of hospitality as a bridge between strangers, a bond in which "lies hidden the idea of humanity and of human fellowship:"

> Hospitality has become a harmless urbane quality in the order of . . . civility, politeness, and table manners. It is on the verge of being regarded as a matter of personality . . . not far removed from the peculiar oblivion spread ever wider by our obsession with the particular and private. If we manage, across some period of time, not to be rude to our friends within our own house . . . then we are deemed hospitable. . . . We forget that properly hospitality has to do with unrecognizable strangers rather than with kith and kin . . . ancient hospitality is firstly and primarily a bond between utter strangers.[2]

Most of us from experience know what real hospitality feels like. It means being received openly, warmly, freely, without the need to earn your keep or prove yourself. An inhospitable space is one in which we feel invisible—or visible but on trial. A hospitable space is alive with trust and good will, rooted in a sense of our common humanity. When we enter such a space we feel worthy, because the host assumes we are. Here there are no preconceptions about how we "should" or "must" be. Here we are accepted for who and what we are. In the words of Henri Nouwen,

> The paradox of hospitality is that it wants to create an emptiness, not a fearful emptiness, but a friendly emptiness where strangers can enter and discover themselves as created free; free to sing their own songs, speak their own languages, dance their own dances; free also to leave and follow their own vocations. Hospitality is not a subtle invitation to adopt the lifestyle of the host, but the gift of a chance for the guest to find his own.[3]

This paradox has special application to our relations in the public life. Hospitality means letting the stranger remain a stranger while offering acceptance nonetheless. It means honoring the fact that strangers already have a relationship—rooted in our common humanity—without having to build one on intimate interpersonal knowledge, without having to become friends. It means valuing the strangeness of the stranger—even letting the stranger speak a language you cannot speak or sing a song you cannot join with—resisting the temptation to reduce the relation to some lowest common denominator, since all language and all music is already human. It means meeting the stranger's needs while allowing him or her simply to be, without attempting to make the stranger over into a modified version of ourselves.

The value of relations between strangers is hard to see in an age so dominated by the norms of intimacy. We assume that relations which lack depth of communication and interpersonal insight are without merit or meaning; and knowing how seldom it is possible to go deep with another person (to say nothing of how risky) we focus our energies on a few people and ignore the rest. So the public, that vast crowd of strangers, becomes a blurred backdrop against which our private dramas are played, and we miss altogether the drama inherent in the public life itself.

The insistence on intimacy undermines the public life, for relations in public will never have that kind of duration and depth. But neither can relations in public remain suspicious and hostile if public life is to flourish. The Christian call to hospitality supports authentic public life, for the hospitable person knows how to relate to the stranger without demanding that the stranger reveal his or her self. This is what Jesus called for—hospitality to the sick and the hungry and the imprisoned without demanding that they become our friends or grateful allies, but hospitality in simple recognition of our unity with them, a unity which is both human and divine. Every hospitable act is an outward and visible sign of our inward and invisible unity, a unity which finds expression in the very root of the word "hospitality," for *hospes* means both host and guest—the two are really one.

Hospitality is especially important because it links the private and the public life, giving us a way to walk between the two realms. The stranger is found in public, but the means of hospitality are private. Hospitality means inviting the stranger into our private space, whether that be the space of our own home or the space of our personal awareness and concern. And when we do so, some important transformations occur. Our private space is suddenly enlarged; no longer tight and cramped and restricted, but open and expansive and free. And our space may also be illumined. Who knows how the presence of the stranger may throw light on some aspect of our lives which we had not seen before—a bias, a misapprehension, a hidden treasure, a gift? Hospitality to the stranger give us a chance to see our own lives afresh, through different eyes.

And when we invite the stranger into our private space, we suddenly become aware of how our private lives have public implications. This is the experience of people who host foreign students in their homes, or participate in programs which allow suburban and inner-city children to change places for a week. When we learn that the stranger has never had a room of his or her own; when we learn that our simple house appears as a palace to the stranger; then we begin to understand how our use of scarce resources is related to the way others are forced to live.

Of course, there are many ways to invite the stranger into our private space. For example, I correspond regularly with a man who is in prison; the program which brought us together is sponsored by a religious organization and is a good illustration of creative hospitality. I have never met this man, I do not know what crime he committed, and I do not expect that he will ever be in my home. He is a stranger. And yet our correspondence brings him into my private life and me into his. I do not know how the relationship feels to him, but I do know that my original emotions were hesitancy, anxiety, even fear about the nature of this stranger I was admitting into my life—sure signs that my precious privacy was being breached and threatened! But as the correspondence continues, my fear drains away as I break through stereotypes of the stranger into the direct and compelling experience of another human being. Again, ministry to strangers does not do them as much good as it does us, in my case creating a greater sense of ease and at-home-ness in the world.

If we are not ready even to reach out by mail, we can practice hospitality by using care when we speak of the stranger in private, a hospitality of the heart. So often we use the cover of privacy to speak words of condemnation which we would not speak in public places—and as we do so we diminish the possibilities of a healthy public life. Children often learn racism in the privacy of their own homes, even though their public experience might not lead them to such attitudes. They learn it because adults hide behind privacy to say things unfit for public consumption. A private language of understanding and compassion can be a great contribution to the public life; it breeds hospitable attitudes towards the stranger even if the stranger is never invited into one's home.

In all of these ways, the stranger of public life becomes the spiritual guide of our private life. Through the stranger our view of self, of world, of God is deepened and expanded. Through the stranger we are given a chance to find ourselves. And through the stranger, God finds us and offers us the gift of wholeness in the midst of our estranged lives, a gift of God and of the public life.

4

Private, Public, and Political
The Vital Links

1

In the last chapter I tried to show that a public life is essential to the spiritual quest. In this chapter I want to argue that public life is equally vital to two other arenas of human experience, the private and the political.

As I turn to examine private and political life, I am not leaving spiritual matters behind, for Christian faith must find expression in both of these other realms. The private life is undergirded by the clear affirmation Christianity gives to the sanctity of the individual; in private a person should find protected freedom for the expression of his or her integrity. If private life is to offer such protections, it will depend heavily on the health of the political process—to say nothing of how politics impinges on the Christian commitment to justice for all. So the subject of this chapter is no less "spiritual" than the last, even if the language seems more "secular."

My thesis is simple. In a society which lacks a healthy public life, both private and political life will suffer. In the absense of a public which knows and cares about itself, private life tends to become obsessive and fearful, while political institutions become centralized, overweening, and even totalitarian. If we want authentic privacy and authentic politics, we must cultivate the public life on which both depend.

2

Earlier, when I defined the public life, I found it useful to contrast public with private. But the two, though different, are not necessarily in opposition. Properly understood, public and private interact, shape one another, depend on each other for their very existence.

Today, we have lost that sense of interdependence. Some of us have lost it through an obsessive search for private values, a search which we mistakenly think requires us to abandon the public realm. And the sense has also been lost among those who have criticized our withdrawal from public relatedness into private autonomy. Many of these critics seem to feel that defense of the public requires denigration of the private; reading them one gets the idea that private life is thoroughly and necessarily diseased. Here is Richard Sennett—one of the most creative advocates of public life—dissecting the "tyrannies of intimacy" which he sees dominating our private lives:

> There are two images which easily come to mind as intimate tyrannies. One is a life limited by children, mortgages on the house, quarrels with one's spouse, trips to the vet, the dentist, the same hours for waking, catching the train to work, returning home . . . the worry over bills—a catalogue of domestic routine soon produces one image of intimate tyranny; it is claustrophobia. Intimate tyranny can also stand for a kind of political catastrophe, the police state in which all one's activities, friends, and beliefs pass through the net of governmental surveillance.[1]

There is a small minority of families which could fairly be compared to totalitarian societies (families, for example, in which spouse-beating or child abuse occurs). But the average family in its daily tedium is not really as bad as a police state. Rhetoric like that is not only unbelievable, it uncritically mirrors the fallacy which dominates our privatistic age—the fallacy of regarding public and private as antithetical, of believing that people must choose one against the other. As Christopher Lasch has noted, "It is the devastation of personal life, not the retreat into privatism, that needs to be criticized and condemned."[2] And that devastation has been caused by a collapse of public values and concern.

Over against Sennett's line of thought we must honor the virtues of private life itself, show how private life can be lived with public needs in mind, and, most important of all, demonstrate that the renewal of public life is essential to the renewal of the private realm. As long as we think of public and private as being in competition, few of us will turn from the pursuit of private values to the defense of public life.

Despite its cultured despisers, the value of private life seems obvious. It offers us the intimacy, the trust, the immediate acceptance which public life seldom provides. ("Home," as Robert Frost once wrote, "is something you somehow haven't to deserve.") The most public of persons needs private life to survive, and to do public work of quality. This much was learned by the activists of the sixties, some of whom burned out in their public roles—and did public violence in the process—because they had failed to practice a private rhythm of renewal. And deeper still, the most public of persons needs private life to live full-round. For the private is not only a realm of comfort against the challenges of public experience: private life contains challenges all its own. Here our capacity for deep and sustained interpersonal relations is tested. Here we face those solitary struggles of the soul in which no one can accompany us, and without which we are not fully human.

Private life is not only an alternative to public life. It is also a life which can be lived in harmony with public claims. We continually make decisions in private which affect the commonweal, as the ecologists (to take but one example) have shown us. When I keep my home warmer than it needs to be, I consume fuel which might help someone else keep warm, or keep a job. When the food I eat is high on the protein chain I contribute to a maldistribution of protein around the world. When I teach my children to be primarily concerned with private gain, I diminish the ranks of public leadership in the rising generation. In all of these areas I have a choice—to lead a private life which recognizes or ignores public need. There is no way for the public to flourish when most people live private life for its own sake.

Perhaps it is not so evident that a healthy public life is necessary for private life to flourish, that many of the problems which vex our private lives require public solutions. Take, for example, the growing American obsession with protecting our homes, our property, and ourselves against criminal invasion. We devote all of our energies to private solutions—lights, locks, alarm systems, "pet" dogs with killer instincts, mace guns small enough to fit a purse—and the more elaborate our private precautions become, the more insecure we grow. We fail to see that private security cannot be assured by private means alone, that without a healthy public life we will remain anxious and unsafe. Where the streets stand empty, no longer host to a steady flow of people in public; where neighbors live in hiddenness, with no sense of connection to one another; where masses mingle in subways under conditions which compel them to ignore one another; in such places criminals can move freely, unobserved, unchecked. And where public consciousness is lacking, even the criminal who is observed will go unchallenged, the victim unaided. The best deterrent to crime against private property and persons is not a home arsenal, or even a skilled and well-financed police force, but the presence of a public which is aware of and cares about itself.

Or take a private problem of a very different sort—the classic difficulties involved in raising teenage children. We have treated this problem as if it were a purely private affair, subject only to the intimate dynamics of the parent-child relationship. But it is also a problem with public dimensions, created in part by our lack of a healthy public life. The typical teenager is struggling to break free from the private circle of family and friends (which, for all its comforts, is also constricting) into a larger world where new freedoms, new versions of the self, can be tried and tested. That is, the teenager seeks a public life, but we have none to offer. Where, for instance, does the adolescent go to relate to adults who are neither parents nor teachers (i.e., not authority figures) but simply fellow citizens? Those few communities which have answers are fortunate indeed. For the most part, our young people are segregated (as are the poor, the elderly, the ill) and such segregation is the antithesis of an open public life. Private psychology can treat the perplexities of youth only to a point; beyond that the remedy lies in a revitalized public realm, as Paul Goodman's evocative words suggest:

> A man has only one life and if during it he has no great environment, no community, he has been robbed of a human right. This loss is especially damaging in growing up, for it deprives outgoing growth, which begins with weaning from Mother and walking out of the house, of the chance of entering upon a great and honorable scene to develop in.[3]

We delude ourselves if we think that private life can be enhanced by retreating from the public realm. The public helps make the private. We cannot have one without the other.

3

A healthy public life would aid not only teenagers but a wide range of other people whose needs are usually interpreted in strictly private psychological terms. The fact is that public life itself offers a kind of therapy which is unattainable in the private sphere. We can understand the deeper connections between public and private by seeing how faith in private therapy has come to substitute for faith in the public realm—and how the substitute has failed.

Philip Rieff points out that the development of private therapy coincided with the rise of industrialization and urbanization—trends which had a corrosive effect on the bonds of community, on our sense of membership in one another.[4] As the shared framework of life crumbled, as people lost the reassuring feelings of purpose and place which that framework provided, therapy arose as a way of helping people gain an identity not dependent upon the common life. The message of the therapeutic motif, broadly conceived, is this: learn to stand on your own two feet. Become autonomous, independent of others. There is no longer any great community to support and guide you—and such a community can never arise again. Only the self remains. As one observer has written:

> Even when they speak of the need for "meaning" and "love," therapists define love and meaning simply as the fulfillment of the patient's

emotional requirements. It hardly occurs to them—nor is there any reason why it should, given the nature of the therapeutic enterprise—to encourage the subject to subordinate his needs and interests to those of others, to someone or some cause or tradition outside himself. Love as self-sacrifice or self-abasement, "meaning" as submission to a higher loyalty—these sublimations strike the therapeutic sensibility as intolerably oppressive, offensive to common sense and injurious to personal health and well-being. To "liberate" humanity from such outmoded ideas of love and duty has become the mission of the post-Freudian therapies and particularly of their converts and popularizers, for whom mental health means the overthrow of "inhibitions" and the nonstop celebration of the self.[5]

Now, it is clear that therapy, the rebuilding of the sense of self, is necessary and useful in some cases. It is also clear that the process of therapy need not be inimical to life in community; that, for example, the movement of persons toward what Jung called "individuation" can give people the inner integrity to enter community as contributing members rather than parasites. But it is also clear that the therapeutic motif is easily perverted into an affirmation of self against the dream-wish of community; that, for example, the process of individuation is often interpreted as a process of pursuing one's own wants and needs without regard to others. And why not, when the community in which our needs might be mutually met is missing and presumed dead?

All around us are clear signs that the bonds of community are weak, even broken; that none of us can depend on community for support in times of crisis; that the "go it alone" goal of therapy is merely realistic. But if this is realism, it is what C. Wright Mills once called "crackpot realism," for it undermines our lives in at least three ways. First, while private therapy provides ways for individuals to cope with difficult conditions, it does nothing to alter the conditions which make coping necessary! It treats symptoms rather than causes, and while we need symptomatic relief from time to time, we have even greater need to eradicate the root disease. Second, the cynicism about community inherent in this "realism" quickly becomes a self-fulfilling prophecy. Such therapy creates individuals so convinced that community is gone, so dependent on private strategies of coping, that they lack will and energy for rebuilding the common life. Third, the dependence on private treatment deprives persons of another, more powerful kind of cure—the therapy of joining together with others to resist the conditions that deform our private lives.

We need to remember, again and again, that many of our private problems are really public issues. And we need to learn how to make the translation. Such is the lesson of the women's movement of the past decade. Women have long wrestled privately with feelings of impotence, uselessness, diminishment—and many of those feelings have been brought to the therapist's office for treatment. But in the past decade women have begun to discover that their pain is not private and idiosyncratic; that it is shared by many other women; that it is created by conditions which culture and society have imposed, the conditions of sexism. And with their dawning awareness of the public dimension of these private problems, women have begun to work in public as a public, supporting one another and generating the collective energy to change the circumstances which create their pain.

In that process, women have discovered the therapy of public life, a treatment more far-reaching than private therapy can ever be. In public, individuals are drawn out of self-obsession into the lives of others—and that is the first step toward finding a healthy self. And in public, persons working together are able to develop the competence and confidence necessary to overcome individual impotence—another step toward psychic well-being. Private therapy is, and will continue to be, important for many individuals; and it, like private life, can be conducted with public needs in mind. But it will always be incomplete without the therapy of public life, which comes from identifying with one another and working together against the circumstances which create private oppression.

Peter Marin has suggested the marks of a therapy which overcomes the distinction between private and public, the premises of a "cure" which would help a person rebuild both the inner life and the outer world:

> First, a simple willingness to accept the existence of an objective reality equal in significance to the self, a reality which literally

. . . objects as we act upon it. Second, a recognition that much of our present pain is the world's pain, the result of living in a catastrophic age in which we do violence to the best parts of our nature. Third, a consciousness of the natural force within us which demands a moral, political, and historical life in the larger world. Fourth, a humility in the presence of that larger world, a respect for the human meaning gathered there by others struggling both in the present and the past. Finally, a recognition that the future depends directly upon the ways we act individually and in community; that it will never be more just, humane, generous, or sustaining than we ourselves are willing to be; and that the therapist and client, in the solitude of their encounter, create together—in how much of the world they admit to their discourse—a part of the social reality which others will later inhabit.[6]

4

To understand our situation in full, we must see that the "therapeutic motif" is found not only in the analyst's office but in other key institutions of our society. Education is a primary example. In the classroom as well as on the couch people are taught to "go it alone" in a society where one can no longer count on community.

There has always been a tension in American education between training for personal advancement and schooling for the commonweal. But the latter—nurturing a sense of peoplehood, of national community, of public life—has always been seen as a prime purpose of our schools, as witness the famous McGuffey Readers which served as text to generations of students in the nineteenth century. Some would argue that this purpose is well served yet today, pointing to the ever-present civics curriculum where students learn of their membership in something larger than themselves.

But scholars who study education know that the formal curriculum of a school is less important than the "hidden curriculum" of educational practices and pressures; they know that what is taught has less impact on students than the way it is taught. No matter what the textbooks may say about our being part of a larger community, the context of education today is not community but conflict and competition, with students being set against one another (and often against their teachers) in the quest for academic rewards. By practicing adversary education, the schools are conveying the "therapeutic" message: you had better learn to go it alone, because in this school (as in this world) no supportive community is available. If that claim sounds excessive, recall for a moment that when students come together to cooperate on a term paper or examination, many schools call it not "community" but "cheating"!

The fact is that most of us cannot imagine, or support, a "communal" form of education. First, we do not believe that people will do the difficult work of learning except under the pressure of competition. We do not believe that excellence in thinking or anything else can be achieved by letting people stimulate each other. If we no longer believe in original sin, we believe in original laziness, whose only antidote is the pressure of others trying to get ahead. Second, even if people were capable of cooperative learning, we would not regard a noncompetitive education as adequate preparation for life. The world is a jungle, we say, and students had better be prepared to fight for their own. This is the therapeutic assumption at work: the great community is gone and will never be available to us again. So the schools turn out a steady stream of young people who have been taught to cope with the collapse of community but never challenged by a vision of community renewed.

Imagine what might happen if we took the phrase "public education" seriously and tried to design an education which could renew the public's life. Such an education would go far beyond memorizing the pledge of allegiance, studying the Constitution, and all the other gestures schools make toward public relatedness and responsibility. An education for public life would teach us to be supportive of and accountable to one another; to deal creatively with conflicting interests; to understand that we are all in this together, and together we sink or swim. It would do so not by preachment and exhortation but through lived experience. It would, for example, design educational tasks which make students interdependent instead of pitting them against one another. In the process, truth would be served, for truth is a very large matter and we have a better chance of embracing it together than alone. And persons would be served as well, for there is no hope for the individual if there is no future for the common life.

5

In considering the relation of private and public life, I have often touched on political life as well, and necessarily so, for private and political life are connected. One of the key functions of the public is to stand between the two, mediating the relations of the isolated individual with the powers of central government. Now I want to look more directly at the way a healthy public life makes possible a healthy politics, first by showing how the public protects the individual from political manipulation, then by showing how it empowers the individual to play a political role.

When Alexis de Tocqueville visited the youthful U.S.A. in the early nineteenth century, he noted that even then we were a nation of joiners. Everywhere he looked people were banding together in voluntary associations—including churches—to share common interests, to accomplish common goals, to express a common faith. And de Tocqueville saw, with uncommon insight, that if the American experiment in democracy were to succeed, it would require the continued health of these voluntary associations, these crucial forms of public life, because democracy requires some way of defending the isolated individual against the tendency of central government to grow larger, stronger, and more domineering.[7] Any power, even in a democratic state, wants to enlarge its domain: it gravitates toward controlling the thought and behavior of every individual in the society—an impossible goal, but one toward which power is ineluctably drawn. The individual who possesses conscience and freedom of thought and action is often anathema to the determinations of political institutions. Such folk rankle and rabble-rouse and resist in ways which make governing more difficult than those who govern might like.

History offers numerous examples of power's tendency to expand its own domain, "totalitarian" societies so-called because of their success in achieving near-total control. One characteristic of every such society is the abolition of public life, the destruction of those settings in which individuals can come out of isolation to become something greater than themselves. For the individual who has a public life is suddenly more than an individual. He or she is now a member of a body, a part of an organic whole. Central power finds it far more difficult to manipulate and manage such corporate beings than to deal with isolated individuals who have no such memberships. Hence, totalitarianism and the absence of an authentic public life are two sides of the same coin. As Hannah Arendt has written, "The principal characteristic of the tyrant was that he deprived the citizen of access to the public realm, where he would show himself, see and be seen, hear and be heard, that he . . . confined the citizens to the privacy of their households."[8]

Of course, the privacy enforced by the tyrant is not real privacy at all. It is more like imprisonment. As public life dwindles, so does the authenticity, the freedom, the richness of the private sphere. In the absence of a healthy public life, the private person stands naked and alone, vulnerable to the impact of whatever leveling powers are abroad in the land.

In our society, constitutional guarantees of individual rights have thus far protected most of us against the worst of governmental incursions into our private life (though there are Americans—for instance, those who most audibly protested the war in Viet Nam—who have found their privacy invaded by an offended officialdom). Nevertheless, our private life has been affected by other leveling powers, notably the powers of commercialism and mass culture. In the most privatized sectors of our society, the middle-class suburbs, there is little variety in the styles of private life, precisely because isolated individuals must turn somewhere for collective meaning, and lacking a culture of local community they turn to the culture conveyed by the mass media and mass market. Thus, the great irony that in these fortresses of rugged individualism one finds homogeneity in everything from furnishings to political opinions. If public life could be renewed in such settings, an interesting reversal would occur. The homogeneity of mass culture would be replaced by the individuality and variety which public interaction creates—for public life, far from being a leveling force, is a context in which pluralism is encouraged, uncontrolled by the monolithic images of commercialism, mass media, or central government.

The ultimate irony in our obsessive pursuit of private life is that no matter how successful such pursuit may be, the human need for a common life, for community, remains powerfully alive; but in a privatized society that need can be met only in fraudulent ways. In our own case, we have the fraudulent community of mass culture, or of white superiority, or of any number of exclusive cults and authoritarian movements which offer people the security of collective memberships. In other cases around the world we have the fraudulent community of totalitarianism itself. What was the Third Reich other than an outcome of the desperate longing for community among people plunged into competitive isolation by an economy run amok?

It would be gross exaggeration to say that America, with our diminished public life, is on the verge of a totalitarian takeover—at least in the sense that persons with governmental power have such a takeover in mind. But the reality of our situation is even more distressing, for if no one is attempting to seize total power we—the public—are laying the groundwork for such an attempt by allowing our public life to wither and die. By focusing our energies on the private and neglecting the public realm we are defaulting on our democratic heritage, yielding our political birthright of government as servant (not master) of the people. We have made a profound mistake in thinking we can have a rich private life under the protection of government without devoting ourselves to the nurture of the public sphere. It will not work. As our problems grow more complex, as the desire for simplistic answers grows, we will see more and more evidence that deTocqueville was a prophet.

6

De Tocqueville saw that the protection of the individual from the invasions of governmental power was not the only reason voluntary associations (and the whole of public life) were essential to a democracy. The process works the other way as well. A healthy public life not only protects people from power, but empowers them to guide government and hold it accountable. Just as the isolated individual is impotent to resist the imposition of central power, so the isolated individual is impotent to direct that power in its course.

But when people band together in public settings, several kinds of empowerment occur. Most obviously, numbers speak. When the streets of Washington are filled with tens of thousands of people protesting a policy decision, the policy makers have to take note. When associations spring up across the country to voice collective sentiments on matters of concern to citizens, those in power (who are sometimes hard of hearing) have to learn to listen. As individuals participate in the public life, their powers not only add up but they multiply. And as people participate in the public life, they are empowered in other ways as well. In particular, they gain confidence and competence in the skills required to function in public, skills which may develop in small and insignificant settings but which enable people to move on to larger circles of public concern.

I recall attending a Sunday school session in a small black church in the rural south. Only four or five people were present, but the meeting functioned strictly according to Robert's Rules of Order. The class president presided, a secretary took notes, and a parliamentarian was available to resolve questions of proper process. The whole scene struck me as overdone. With so few people involved, would it not make sense to proceed in a more casual manner? When I raised that question with the pastor he informed me with some vigor that in such classes disenfranchised people had a rare, even singular opportunity to learn how to function in a political setting—how to get one's concerns on the agenda, how to argue one's case, how to practice negotiation and compromise in a conflict situation. He argued—and rightly so—that I had witnessed the formation of citizens, of public people, who were learning skills and gaining the confidence necessary to function effectively in political settings. The pastor's hope was that such modest experiences as these would equip his people for life in larger and more crucial public settings, settings where issues of justice for the black community were being decided. That his hope is not illusory is demonstrated by the long history of blacks emerging from the church to make a forceful claim on America's political process.

As we come to understand the centrality of voluntary associations in the public health of our society, and as we look around at the large number of such associations which dot the American landscape, it is tempting to conclude that the public life is not nearly as threadbare as I have claimed. Readers will think of instances in which people act together with vigor and discipline, when (for example) a federal judge orders school integration through busing, or when a planning agency proposes to build low-income housing in a suburban neighborhood. Then it becomes clear that there are matters of vital interest to all—the schools, our neighborhoods, the relations of the races, the extent of the law's authority. Then, it would seem, a public life is generated.

But such outbursts of "public" activity are not deeply public at all. They may, in fact, be symptoms of how little public life we have. First, the events which arouse public interest are often events which threaten to bring diverse elements of the population into more frequent contact with each other, as through school busing or public housing. If genuine public life means anything, it means the ability to live with diversity, not ignore it or try to gerrymander it out of view. These episodes of so-called public sentiment are riddled with the fear of diversity, which itself is a symptom of our disease.

Second, events such as these occur only sporadically, while genuine public life is a continuing affair. The public life depends on regular encounters—most of them not overtly political—between strangers who cross each other's paths, become accustomed to each other's presence, and come to recognize their common claims on the society. When the balance of life shifts heavily toward the private and these regular encounters diminish, people come into public only in moments of crisis, moments which usually set stranger against stranger in sudden and unexpected conflicts of interest. There is an inverse relation between the health of public life and the need to conduct politics by crisis: the less public life there is, the more likely that conflicts will reach the crisis point before they are dealt with. A healthy public life creates a steady flow of information and opinions so that threats to one's interests are perceived and responded to gradually and in advance, thus increasing the chance that interests can be altered or accommodation reached.

Third, the way we frame these conflicts over (for example) busing and housing belies the notion that they reveal a lively public life. We define them as "zero-sum" games in which each gain for one side is a loss for the other; a game, that is, in which some must lose in order for some to win; a game where it is inconceivable that everyone might emerge with a victory of some sort. A genuine public life would begin with the premise that there are victories for the whole which are greater than a victory for any of its parts. We would understand that we are members of one another; that the social order will be secure for our own life, liberty and pursuit of happiness only if it is secure for others as well. We would know, for example, that when we force low-income housing out of our community we are not solving the problem but merely postponing the day of reckoning. Worse still, we are allowing the pressures of inequity and resentment to build to a point where no rational solution will suffice. The foundation of public life is the tenacious faith that we are in this together and can find ways for everyone to win. This is not a faith which accompanies many outbursts of so-called public activity these days.

In fact, a growing number of the voluntary associations in which de Tocqueville placed such hope reflect a loss of this public faith, the faith that we all can win. I refer, of course, to the single-issue groups which now dot the American scene, groups whose philosophies and strategies deform the public realm.

The voluntary associations which contribute most to our political health are those with broad-based concerns, those which (like the church) allow people to come together, to share opinions, to influence each other's thinking on a broad range of issues. The health of a democracy is premised on the assumption that the population will not be divided along single-issue lines; that there will be a variety of cross-cutting divisions between us; that you and I will be on the opposite side of some causes but on the same side of others; and that in this way we will come to see that we are related despite our differences.

But single-issue groups separate people along absolute lines. They take one concern and make it not only paramount but apocalyptic. If you are not against (or for) voluntary abortion; if you are not for (or against) gun control; if you are not against (or for) nuclear power; then you are among the damned. For such groups and the people who join them, the world has only one moral boundary. And with this kind of thinking the idea of a public with complex and interlaced concerns is lost. Now there can be no accommodation, no compromise, no balancing of interests, no looking beneath the conflict for a creative "third way." Now the public disappears, and in its place emerge the righteous and the sinners, separated out by groups who would play the role of Lord on judgment day.

7

It is no accident that I began using religious imagery to characterize the excesses of single-issue politics. For our history offers many examples of political fanaticism clothed in spirituality. Indeed, some would argue that spiritual intensity is especially apt to give rise to political extremism, and they would be able to offer examples from the contemporary scene. So in a book where I argue that religious persons and institutions should aid in the renewal of public life, I need to face these dangers and to ask how they can be avoided.

The main danger of "spiritual politics" is, of course, the denial of pluralism. When a religious group is able to translate its program into political terms, it is tempted to impose its own version of righteousness on everyone; hence, the wisdom of the Constitution which dictates that the United States shall not have an established state church. I would not breach the "wall of separation" between church and state. But I would insist that a healthy state, a healthy political process, is grounded in a healthy public life, and that the church can do much to nurture that life without attempting to sieze political power.

Still, the spectre remains. How does the body of Christ relate to the body politic? With what purposes and intentions does the church enter the public realm? Some will fear campaigns of Christian triumphalism, efforts to bring the world and all its heathen into the bosom of the church. I want to dissociate myself from this notion of Christian mission, and to indicate another way of thinking about the role of the church in the world. In my view, the mission of the church is not to enlarge its membership, not to bring outsiders to accept its terms, but simply to love the world in every possible way—to love the world as God did and does. The body of Christ is a network of organic connections between people, connections which make one's joy another's joy, one's suffering another's suffering. In this sense, everyone, Christian or otherwise, is included in the body of Christ—included not within an organizational framework or a theological point of view, but included within a community of compassion. I do not belive the church enters the public realm to aggrandize itself, but to glorify God; and God is glorified as we manifest the unity in which we were created without dishonoring the diversity we have become. If we are able to love the world, that will be the best demonstration of the truth which the church has been given.

Another feature of Christian experience which protects pluralism is encounter with the vastness of God. At the heart of any authentic religious experience is recognition that God's nature is too huge, God's movement too deep, ever to be comprehended by a single conception or point of view. Every contemplative knows that our theologies are imperfect reflections of God's truth, that our religious institutions are deformed approximations of the shape God would give our corporate life. Paul had such facts in mind when he wrote that "we have this treasure in earthen vessels, to show that the transcendent power belongs to God and not to us" (I Cor. 4:7). God's truth is singular and eternal, but the forms in which we give it expression are as finite and fragile as clay pots, and we must always be ready to break them open on behalf of a larger vision of truth.

So Christian experience protects pluralism with the recognition that we need many angles of vision, many ways of reflecting and refracting the light of the Spirit in our midst. Once we think that our conception of God *is* God, we have committed idolatry. The diversity of the public, its many voices and points of view, is to be treasured by those who are seekers after truth.

This does not mean that one is free to remain in a state of indecision, as so many liberal Christians are today. There is a vast difference between openness to new truth and merely being empty-headed. In fact, to refuse to take a stand is to remove oneself from the struggle toward truth which genuine pluralism involves. To say "maybe this, maybe that" is to remain above the fray, to refuse to make one's contribution to the dialectic of truth-finding which can go on in the public sphere. In this way not only do we fail to contribute to others' thinking, we also fail to make ourselves vulnerable to their insights. Genuine pluralism does not mean "anything goes." It means that every point of view is put forward for corporate testing, and personal openness means being responsive to the results of that test.

Another principle of Christian faith which protects pluralism is found in the idea of "covenant." For to be in covenant with the Lord, to be the people of God, is not to receive power and privilege and the right to domineer over others. Instead, covenant means the acceptance of weighty obligations to a Lord who demands that we "do justice, love mercy, and walk humbly with thy God."

If the church in America accepted the true covenant, it would not thereby declare itself superior to the civil society, to Jews and Muslims and nonbelievers. Instead, it would be accepting the awesome obligation to serve as a channel of reconciliation in a world in love with divisions. By accepting the covenant, the church would also be accepting God's judgment of its life, for steady and uncompromising love is beyond the reach of any institution. By accepting the covenant the church would not be laying claim to some fixed and final state of salvation, but would be entering upon a continual process of faithfulness, failure, forgiveness, and the grace to be faithful again. By accepting the covenant the church would proclaim not its mastery over the world but its servanthood—to God, to humankind, and to the vision of a peaceable kingdom.

Finally, it is this image of servanthood which keeps authentic

Christian faith from seeking political dominance. For this is the image of Jesus himself, the one who came not as a warrior bent on seizing the reins of power but as a powerless servant, armed only with love. It is in this image that we find the paradox of Christian involvement in public life, the paradox which says that there is power in powerlessness. As Jesus taught with his life, we are to eschew the world's ways of power so that the power of God's reconciling love may fill our lives. It is not the church's task to "Christianize" those who do not see things our way, but to live out the truth we are given—the truth that underneath our diversity we are one. In this reconciliation we seek not the obliteration of human differences—for those differences give us a fuller look at the many sides of truth—but a deepening of each person's integrity. We will find the common ground of public life not by destroying our particularity but by pursuing it, pursuing it to the depths where we encounter the ground of being which gave rise to and sustains us all.

5

Teaching the Public Life I
Scarcity and Abundance

1

By now, I hope I have established what the public life is, why it is important, and why Christians should care about its health. If I have, one major question begs to be answered: What can the churches do to aid in the rediscovery, renewal, reinvention of the public life?

One answer to that question is implicit in everything said thus far. Christians must study the nature and functions of the public life, and come to understand how the public life bears on Christian concerns for individual growth toward God and the establishment of God's kingdom on earth. But that, though essential, is only a bare beginning, only the foundation for further effort. In the next four chapters, I will explore ways the church might mobilize its members (and people outside its walls) on behalf of the public life—by teaching a public theology, by practicing a public psychology, and by creating public space through corporate and personal mission.

This chapter and the next, on teaching a public theology, make two assumptions. One is that preaching and teaching are major tools of Christian mission, that to preach or teach about public life is a way of "doing something." Second, I assume that theology—done in a lively way which addresses people's needs—is capable of moving people not only toward new ways of viewing the world, but also toward new ways of being and acting in it. That is, I do not share the cynicism of some activists about the efficacy of "the word." Of course, many words are uttered stillborn, but that is the fault of speaker and listener, not of the word. The church is a community of the Word, and if we can listen closely enough to the word God speaks to us (and that is one function of theology), we can make that word flesh in our own lives.

I have already explored one theological theme which would help sustain our public life—the place of the stranger in our spiritual growth. The problem in trying to develop further themes is that there are far too many to treat in the brief span of a book. So I have chosen only two, hoping to develop each in some depth. I chose these two because they correspond to two major problems of public experience—the problem of scarce resources (the focus of this chapter) and the problem of conflict (which I take up in the next). Our fears about scarcity and conflict cause withdrawal from the public realm. If the church, through its preaching and teaching, could transform our fears into energy for engagement, it would have made a major contribution to the renewal of public life.

It is obvious that the public life involves the problem of scarce resources: a public comes into being partly to deal with scarcity, and scarcity remains a major item on every public's agenda. Even at the most basic levels of public interaction we are continually engaged in the distribution of scarce resources; as we pass on the sidewalk, you get your half and I get mine. Faced with an inadequate supply of, say, jobs or building lots or money for public projects, we look to public mechanisms to solve the problem. And today, of course, scarcity and abundance have become the terms of a global struggle for justice in a world where the "haves" have more than enough while the "have nots" lack what is needed to survive. With predictions of dwindling natural resources, with growing pessimism over technology's ability to provide what we need, even the "haves" begin to feel fear, and are driven to consume and hoard still more, thus further imbalancing the scales of equity. All of this is obvious and well known.

Perhaps it is not so well known that scarcity and abundance are also basic terms in Christian spirituality. There is a direct relation between our state of spiritual awareness, our awareness of God's abundance, and our ability to respond to scarcity in the public realm. The Gospel sees abundance where the world sees scarcity, and scarcity where the world sees abundance. Such a faith can help sustain us in public life, since we often retreat from the public into the private sphere to gather and protect an abundance for ourselves. But in gathering material abundance we will find spiritual scarcity, while in sharing material scarcity with the larger community we discover spiritual abundance. Or so the Gospel claims, a claim I explore in this chapter.

2

David Potter has argued that democracy and abundance go hand-in-hand.[1] If a land lacks ample resources, democracy may never take root; Potter believes that America's political system would never have matured had this country's natural abundance not promised more than enough to go around. But once established, democracy fosters the entrepreneurial spirit which empowers people to develop the resources which are available, to multiply the measure of abundance. Potter believes we are mistaken to impose the democratic model upon countries which lack our natural wealth; in situations of material insecurity, he claims, the democratic process will break down.

The same can be said of the public life, that central component of democracy. Although public life deals with the distribution of scarce resources, the public process tends to fall apart when resources become *too* scarce. For example, as cities become more crowded and street or sidewalk space grows scarce, our pleasure at being in public declines and we avoid the streets (i.e., the public) whenever possible. Or in a national emergency, when information and time to act are suddenly in short supply, we suspend public processes and put massive powers in the hands of the central government.

We need to understand these connections between public life and scarcity/abundance because the fact and the fear of scarcity bear heavily on our willingness to live public lives. When there is plenty to go around, life in public is pleasant. In such times we have no reason to fear the public life since it is unlikely that we will have to fight for our needs or wants. In times of abundance, we can have the best of both worlds—a private life of comfort and a public life in which conflict is at a minimum.

But today, with real scarcity in some areas and the fear of scarcity in others, private comfort is threatened and public life becomes threatening—especially to those who are unaccustomed to scarcity and to fighting for what they need. It is a double bind. On the one hand, scarcity threatens our private resources, and the only durable solutions are in the public realm. On the other hand, scarcity makes public conflict inevitable and often bitter. The same conditions which make a public response necessary also make us afraid of entering the public realm.

Many of us try to find private solutions to the problem of scarce resources. We attempt to beat inflation by sending more members of the family to work. We try to stem the rising rate of crime by fortifying our homes with locks and weapons. We try to guard against the catastrophic costs of serious illness by demanding more fringe benefits from our employers. We may even hoard food staples or fuel against the day when they will be unavailable in the open market.

But, as we have seen before, private solutions tend to exacerbate public problems. Hoarding diminishes the general supply; private health insurance allows medical costs to keep rising; the fortress approach to crime further isolates individuals from the public connectedness which could curb crime; growth in private purchasing power among those who already have enough only stimulates the inflationary cycle. Private solutions to the problem of scarce resources only make the resources scarcer. The greater the scarcity, the more tense becomes the public scene. And the more tense the public, the more difficult it becomes for people to look together for public solutions.

I do not think we can exaggerate the extent to which affluent Americans are caught in this vicious circle. It is said that if the earth were a global village of one hundred people, six of them would be Americans, and those six would have over one-third of the village's income. In such a village everyone would be aware of this fact; what impact would that awareness have on peoples' behavior? The ninety-four people who had to subsist on two-thirds of the income would surely be furious at the remaining six. And the six would surely be afraid of having their possessions, if not their lives, taken from them. The six would be unlikely to participate fully and freely in the public life. Instead, they would arm themselves, hide away as best they could, and develop elaborate rationalizations or avoidance mechanisms to deal with their "good fortune." And that is exactly what well-to-do Americans have done, not only in relation to the Third World but also with their neighbors in poverty here at home.

The ultimate spectre of what scarcity can do to public life is glimpsed in a chilling study by Colin Turnbull of an African mountain people called the Ik.[2] Once a close-knit tribe of hunters and gatherers, the Ik were suddenly denied access to the land which had sustained them—it was converted into a national park. Their source of abundance dried up overnight, and since they were not taught another way of life, they could only scratch out a living on the margins. Within the span of two or three generations, they underwent a tragic transformation from community to a collection of avaricious individuals, each out for him or herself with no regard for anyone else. Adults stole from each other, even from the sick and dying. Hoarding was common, even when one's relative or neighbor was in need. Parents allowed infants to blunder into burning campfires—a child needs to learn that life is harsh, and if the child should die there would be one less mouth to feed. The Ik had reached that point where scarcity became so severe that every pretense of public concern was abandoned.

Our own society, whose scarcities are modest by comparison, already shows tendencies in this direction. Though most of us would rescue an infant from bodily injury if we were on the scene, we blithely ignore high rates of infant mortality on rural reservations and in urban ghettos. How would we behave if genuine scarcity were to become our lot?

3

To develop a theology of scarcity, we must first understand that not all scarcity is an "objective" problem. Some of it is, of course; those people who perished today for want of enough to eat died of objective causes. But much scarcity is artificially induced, caused not by a real lack of resources but by our attitude toward the resources that are available. Indeed, even those people who starved to death today were, in one sense, murdered by other peoples' attitudes. Their lives were sacrificed either to the wants of those who consume more food than their fair share, or to the wants of those who exploit cheap land and labor for purposes more profitable than feeding hungry people.

In one way or another, almost every instance of scarcity is caused by subjective factors as much or more than by objective ones. Diamonds are expensive not simply because they are rare in nature, but because we somehow decided that diamonds are desirable objects to own. The human body has an objective need for protein, but the desire to get that protein from steak rather than beans is a subjective choice—and more protein would be available to the poor if the rich would eat more beans and less steak. In some cases of scarcity, a good may be available in abundance, but the fear that it will become scarce (however groundless the fear) causes people to hoard the item, thus bringing about the very scarcity that was feared! The classic illustration is a "bank run." A bank may be perfectly sound but if word travels that it lacks assets to cover deposits, people will rush to withdraw their money and soon the bank will, in fact, be unable to meet its obligations.

The subjectivity of scarcity is especially striking when we look at nonmaterial goods, goods which are available in infinite supply but which we—by our attitudes—make scarce as diamonds and as much the object of competition. There is an old popular song which says "the best things in life are free," but the scarcity mentality has taken even these things and made them costly. I want to show how this strange phenomenon is both a cause and a consequence of our diminished public life.

Take "entertainment" as an example. Entertaining and being entertained are clearly human goods; life is dull without them. And just as clearly, people are capable of entertaining themselves and others in an infinite variety of ways. Entertainment is abundant in human nature. But this abundant good has become increasingly scarce in our lives not because some genetic mutation has deprived us of the capacity to entertain, but because we have come to define entertainment as something one buys from the entertainment industry. For many people, entertainment in the home means television. Television costs money. For many people, entertainment outside the home means professional sports, or theater. These too cost money. As we become more dependent on entertainment produced by the industry, we become a passive audience, losing touch with our own capacity to entertain ourselves. And as we lose touch with our own abundant ability to entertain, we are compelled to buy more and more of this good in the marketplace. It is a vicious circle, the circle of scarcity.

What has happened, of course, is the institutionalization of entertainment. Our society has professionalized the task of entertaining itself and has created a cadre of persons who earn their living by doing just that. And the key to the survival of any profession is to persuade people that they cannot produce the good or service for themselves; the product must be kept scarce, the price kept high, and the producers kept in business.

In this process the public life is undermined, for many of the nonmaterial goods which are kept in short supply are not only goods which the public can generate, they are goods which provide the stuff of public life to begin with! Entertainment, again, is an excellent example, for part of the thrill of public life is the entertainment it provides. The public life is the human comedy enacted; coming together in public places, people amuse themselves. When public life is thriving people are not drawn into it primarily for the sober business of debating priorities and dealing with conflict; such business as this cannot be the prime or sole activity of the public. No, people are most powerfully drawn into public because it is an interesting place to be, a place full of color and texture and variety. At its best, the public life has the quality of a carnival or fair which people *want* to attend—and as they spend time enjoying each other, they are empowered to do the more difficult public business. In fact, the root meaning of "entertain" is "to hold mutually" or "to hold intertwined," that is, to bring people together in a common body. As people feel the bonds created by the entertaining side of public life, their capacity to deal with public conflict is strengthened.

4

Entertainment is not the only nonmaterial good which we have made artificially scarce. There are many others, and each case of contrived scarcity diminishes the public life. Take, for example, the good called "caring."

Within each of us there is a capacity to respond to people in need. For millennia, people have turned to each other for various sorts of aid, and as we do so—and receive response—our common bond, our public life, is strengthened. But in our century caring has become increasingly professionalized and institutionalized. If a friend comes with some sort of "psychological disturbance" we often feel inadequate to help, and will withdraw or refer the friend to a minister or counselor instead. The very terms we use to describe our troubles (chronic depression, paranoia, schizophrenia) are so technical, so weighty, as to suggest that no mere amateur should even attempt to help. And that is no accident, for those are the terms promoted by a profession which protects itself by keeping caring in short supply. When professionals hoard their knowledge, public life is diminished no less than when consumers hoard fuel and food. In both cases private interests are promoted at public expense.

The scarcity of care in our society results not only from the self-serving behavior of some professionals. It results also from the fact that there are some human problems which the public does not wish to face or even acknowledge. By institutionalizing these problems we meet our need to have them kept out of sight, out of mind. Prisons, mental hospitals, homes for the aged, wards for the dying —all of these serve to remove problem people from public view. Our squeamishness conspires with professional self-interest to keep these human needs hidden.

Here is another vicious circle. As our sense of relatedness began to break down in an urbanizing, industrializing society, human care became professionalized. With professionalization, our own sense of adequacy to care for one another begins to diminish, and feeling inadequate we withdraw from those places where we might learn to care—thus further weakening our sense of relatedness. As we remove human needs from public view, we remove another factor which might make a public out of a crowd. The public emerges in part around the meeting of mutual needs, and a public is sustained as it finds within itself the resources to meet those needs. It is especially tragic that we have made human care artificially scarce, for it is in caring and being cared for that people discover the bonds of relatedness on which the public life depends.

Another example of artificial scarcity which undermines public life involves education of the young. Education is meant to be a public function, a task in which the elders express and foster a common culture by passing it along to the rising generation. At earlier times in our society that function was performed not only by the schools but by families and neighbors and employers; that is, by a complex network of youth-adult relationships. But now that network has broken down, and we relegate the education of the young almost wholly to the schools.

The schools, standing alone, cannot do the job. The larger community, knowing that the job is not being done, doubts and distrusts the schools—because they are failing to do an impossible task well. But will the schools relinquish parts of the task, encouraging other institutions in the community to play their part? No, because by controlling the marketing of education, the schools maintain their power: that is the logic of scarcity.

A few years ago, innovative educators proposed a "voucher system" of education. By this plan, tax money for education would not go to the schools but to the parents of school age children (in the form of "vouchers"). With these vouchers parents would be able to put their children in the kind of educational situation they felt best—perhaps a conventional school, perhaps a religious school, perhaps an apprenticeship, perhaps a work-study program. The idea was not only to increase the citizen's freedom of choice but also to spread the educational function more widely through the community. Of course, most educators did not support the plan. If adopted, it would destroy their monopoly.

When we give the schools a monopoly on education, not only do we make teaching and learning artificially scarce, we also deprive the public of a function which helps make it a public. If we could create situations in which a wide variety of adults could share what they know with the young, we would nurture that sense of common culture and common calling so essential to the public life.

So, through attitudes and institutions, we transform abundance into scarcity—not only in our economic life, but also in such areas as entertainment, human caring, and education. The reader can add examples of his or her own. The question is, where can we find a source of vision and perspective which will overturn our assumptions about scarcity and abundance and, in so doing, help revive our public life?

5

Such a source, I think, is found in Christian experience and theology. I want not only to spell out the theory, but to show how well the theory corresponds to the lived experience of public life.

Christians, as Paul said, are to be "in but not of the world." We are to take responsibility for the world's reality, but we need not accept the world's definition of what that reality is: in the book of Acts, the early Christians are described as those "who have turned the world upside down." (17:6). Nowhere is this Christian counterculture more vividly revealed than in Jesus' teachings about scarcity and abundance. Time and again, Jesus inverts the problem of scarcity, toppling the conventional wisdom. Where the worldly mind trusts material abundance, Jesus points to its fragility and undependability:

> Do not lay up for yourselves treasures on earth, where moth and rust consume and where thieves break in and steal, but lay up for yourselves treasures in heaven, where neither moth nor rust consumes and where thieves do not break in and steal. For where your treasure is, there will your heart be also. (Matt. 6:19–21)

Not only is material abundance precarious, but our anxiety about getting and holding it blocks us from receiving the abundance of the Spirit:

> Therefore I tell you, do not be anxious about your life, what you shall eat or what you shall drink, nor about your body, what you shall put on. . . . And which of you by being anxious can add one cubit to his span of life? . . . Consider the lilies of the field, how they grow, they neither toil nor spin; yet I tell you, even Solomon in all his glory was not arrayed like one of these. . . . Seek first his kingdom and his righteousness, and all these things shall be yours as well. (Matt. 6:25–33)

Like so many teachings of Jesus, his comments on scarcity and abundance take the form of paradox. The more material abundance we have or seek, the more likely we are to starve from scarcity of the Spirit. But if we can let go of our anxiety about material scarcity, a great abundance of the Spirit will be opened to us. There is an obvious parallel here to Jesus' counsel that when we seek life we will lose it, but when we lose our life in God, we will find it. Spiritual truth is always paradoxical. That which we lust and strive for so often eludes us. But when we let go of our obsessive desires, we may find ourselves in possession of something good—something given as a gift, unexpected and unearned. So it is with the gift of abundance in our lives.

Sometimes this abundance comes directly to the individual, filling the heart, in silence, in solitude, in a setting of great beauty, or in music that moves deep within us. But often in Christian experience abundance comes in community as people share their lives and their problems and their resources. The individual is incomplete (i.e., scarce) without others, but as people act in ways which acknowledge their relatedness, they are given the abundance of community itself.

The most memorable New Testament account of this experience is found in the book of Acts where the story of the first Pentecost is told. The people had gathered for worship when "they were all filled with the Holy Spirit and began to speak in tongues as the

Spirit gave them utterance" (Acts 2:4). Further on, the writer tells of one outcome of this experience:

> Now the company of those who believed were of one heart and soul, and no one said that any of the things which he possessed was his own, but they had everything in common. And with great power the apostles gave their testimony to the resurrection of the Lord Jesus, and great grace was upon them all. There was not a needy person among them, for as many as were possessors of lands or houses sold them, and brought the proceeds of what was sold and laid it at the apostles' feet; and distribution was made to each as had any need. (Acts 4:32–35)

I am impressed not only by the experience of speaking in tongues (an experience of spiritual abundance which could—and sometimes does—remain private and esoteric) but by the way that experience overflowed into material sharing. Here, the Spirit filled lives with such a sense of plenty that people were freed and empowered to share their wealth with those in need. And as people share what they have, they are further opened to the abundance of the Spirit; surely this was the outward spiral of growth in the early church.

In the Christian experience, the movement of the Spirit is thus a link between the private and the public realms. The same Spirit which comes to us in such deeply inward and mysterious ways as to defy rational communication also comes to us as an outreaching bond of love and obligation to brothers and sisters around the earth. The same Spirit which melts and molds our secret hearts also shapes visible, historical communities of sharing and commitment. In the early church, speaking in tongues was not a private practice to be coveted by an initiated few. It became articulate as an active and public language of love. In that language, the words "scarcity" and "abundance" are not poles of opposition, the one to be fled, the other sought, but reciprocal realities. By sharing in scarcity we find authentic abundance.

This paradox is no mere spiritual theory. It is not found only in biblical testimony but in our own experience as well. It is the paradox which explains why the private life of affluent Americans is haunted by the spectre of scarcity. We are obsessed with personal gain. We devote so much time and energy to pursuing our own well-being that nothing is left for the public life. Given the enormous investment we make in securing our private fortunes, why should we be so anxious about them? Because in giving our self-interest priority, in declaring our independence from the common life, we become not strong but weak and vulnerable. We know that we have set ourselves apart, that we are pulling for no one and no one is pulling for us—and we fear the day when we cannot pull for ourselves. So, private life in acquisitive society is shot through with scarcity. We are scarce in support, scarce in the satisfaction that cooperation and mutual aid can bring—but abundant in the fear that comes as we realize how alone we are.

Such fears are assuaged by a healthy public life. A functioning public creates abundance not only by finding ways to ration food or fuel in times of shortage so that everyone has a fair share. More important, a healthy public gives people the sense of belonging to a community of support, the sense that whatever scarcities the future may bring, the public will be able to cope. A tankful of gas or a cellar full of food is abundance of a temporary sort, for we know it will run out, that "moth and rust" will corrupt. But to belong to a community that cares, a public that knows how to distribute resources with equity—that is to know real abundance. I still recall the sudden and surprising sense of public life which emerged in the early seventies during the first of the recent gasoline shortages. Commuters accustomed to driving to work in their own cars formed car pools which not only saved gas but gave neighbors and co-workers a chance to know each other. As so often happens in emergencies, the shortage was transformed into the abundance that comes from people sharing, the abundance that comes when fear of isolation is vanquished by the knowledge that we can work together.

But once we became accustomed to scarce and costly fuel we returned to our private habits, one to a car. A deeper and more sustained crisis of scarcity may force us to change our habits again, but our basic need is to re-vision the very problem of scarcity and abundance. Such a vision is provided by Christian faith. By teaching the paradox of scarcity and abundance the church could help people make more sense of what is happening around them and see what kind of response is required.

6

The paradox of scarcity and abundance is shown again in the myth of America's origins. The whites who settled in this country saw themselves moving from a land of scarcity to a land of abundance, from a starving exile in Egypt to the promised land of milk and honey. Here was more of everything: physical space, religious freedom, natural resources, individual opportunity. And we, looking back on the beginnings of the American experiment, also imagine it as a time of abundance—an abundance of spirit and vision and common enterprise which seems sorely lacking in our own time.

But the fact of the matter is that white America began in a kind of scarcity. The Europeans who settled here came to a land with great but undeveloped potential. The resources were present, but transforming them into the things which sustain life was an arduous and risky task. The whites who settled here left a country abundant with culture and arrived in a land where there was no culture with which they could identify. They left communities where the body politic was well developed and came to a land where a new body had to be born, with all the attendant pains. Tragically, those white settlers soon fell into a bloody struggle for sovereignty with the native Americans whose land it was—and there is no better evidence of the unconscious assumption of scarcity which the settlers brought to this land of abundance than this warfare, whose premise is the sense that there was not enough to go around.

Why, then, does the myth hold that America began in abundance? Why did the white settlers, and why do we, see abundance in the midst of the rigors and deprivations of those early days? Precisely because of the paradox. Precisely because it is in the midst of scarcity that abundance is to be found. There is deep truth to a myth which finds social and psychological plenty in the midst of physical hardships and cultural limitations. It is our own time of material comfort and mass culture which gives rise to feelings of social and psychological scarcity.

The true abundance of early America comes not from cheap and plentiful land. It comes, instead, from the collective commitment and effort to turn that land to productive use. The abundance which our myth finds in seventeenth and eighteenth century American life is not a result of agriculture and industry. It is, instead, a result of hope and vision and the public effort to bring that vision into being. That vision was flawed, to be sure, and neither the "public effort" nor its fruits included all the people; those are tragic facts of our history whose implications are still with us in the lives of native Americans and Afro–Americans. But for those allowed to share the vision and the efforts and the re-wards, abundance was indeed found in the midst of scarcity.

The roots of the paradox are found partly in human psychology. There is something in us which takes more satisfaction in the striving than in the achievement, something which finds more fulfillment in striving together than alone. But those psychological tendencies need to be triggered or evoked by a great myth, a myth which gives shape and meaning to such struggles as the settlers faced. It is not incidental that the myth which shaped white America's early awareness of itself was rooted in the Bible, a Bible which continually finds abundance where scarcity seems to prevail. The Europeans who came to this country brought with them a cultural tendency to see things through biblical eyes. And it is through those same eyes—now opened and clarified by God's judgment on our injustice—that we may re-vision the sources of abundance in our own times.

In the midst of material abundance, our lives have become cramped and pinched. As both cause and consequence of that fact, we lack a vital public life. If we had such a life, we would not experience social and psychological scarcity. But feeling the scarcity as we do, we revert to private strateges, retreating from the public life where our common needs might be met. The church could exercise a ministry of singular importance by helping people re-vision our situation in biblical terms. We need to see that we are in an exile of our own making, in captivity to an affluence and a greed which separate us one from another and cut us off from the sources of common abundance. We need to be led out of that captivity toward a land of plenty in which common vision, common effort, and common sharing of the fruits create a genuine abundance in the midst of scarcity. We need to be led from our private poverty into the plenty of public life.

6

Teaching the Public Life II
Conflict, Compassion, and the Way of the Cross

1

It is possible for the public to generate abundance. But until we learn how to do it consistently we will suffer the clash of self-interests as people fight over scarcity. There is joy in public life, the joy of finding ourselves at one. But that sense of the kingdom comes only occasionally. Meanwhile, public experience will include conflict, tension, and pain.

The church must speak to this problem in its preaching and teaching, not only because the fear of pain and conflict drives many from the public realm, but also because the transformation of suffering is at the heart of the Gospel message. Jesus preached atonement, at-one-ment, the unity of all people in the providence of God. He preached and lived the public life at its deepest reaches. And doing so, he threatened those who fed on division and disunity; his message of love created conflict which led to death on the cross. But Jesus' love did not fail, nor God's love in him, and because of his faithfulness his cross led to resurrection, a resurrection of hope which Christians can carry into the conflicts of public life.

Any theology of public life must confront public conflict and the pain it produces. And such a theology must point to the promise of Christian faith: that when we respond to conflict with compassion, even on the cross, we will be resurrected and given new life.

2

Anyone with public experience knows the pain it can bring. Abrasion is inevitable, for this is the arena where seemingly incompatible needs and interests struggle for priority. Even when accommodation is the goal, there is stress along the way as conflicting claims are asserted and each camp insists on the merits of its case. Patience curdles, polite smiles grow tight, weariness mounts, and the temptation builds to declare all-out war or retreat to private solutions.

Worse still, the public is a realm of false promises and betrayals. In the course of reaching accommodation, marriages of convenience are often formed, and these are no more stable or enduring than their literal counterparts. When it becomes more convenient to marry someone else, divorce comes quickly and without warning. Skepticism and cynicism build as we wonder whom we can count on in public.

Perhaps most devastating of all, we often feel that our inner reality, our sense of self, is twisted and misunderstood by others as we play our public roles. People form images of us which are alien and even damaging to our private pictures of ourselves. Negative images leave us feeling judged and vulnerable, while images of adulation lead us away from our own reality (as when we say that public person has begun "to believe his own press"). In either case, the result is self-alienation, the struggle with a caricature of one's self.

In all these ways public life is notorious for its harshness, for its capacity to crush people under the wheels of interminable effort, of intractable problems, of public opinion. We often say that to function effectively in public one must have a "thick skin," a kind of toughness which can resist grinding. Christianity, on the other hand, is often regarded as a soft and sentimental way of looking at the world. "Love," that central commandment of Christian faith, seems far removed from the reality, and even the potential, of public experience. The Christian in public is regarded as a lamb among wolves—a quick meal for those whose appetites know no ethical limits.

When Richard Sennett writes about the damage done to our public life by the ideology of intimacy he could well be writing about the popular view that it is impossible to follow Christian faith in the public sphere:

> The crisis of public culture in the last century taught us to think about the harshness, constraints, and difficulties which are the essence of the human condition in society as overwhelming. We may approach them through a kind of passive, silent spectatorship, but to challenge them, to become enmeshed in them, is thought to be at the expense of developing ourselves. The development of personality today is the development of the personality of a refugee . . . what kind of personality develops through experiences of intimacy? Such a personality will be molded in the expectation, if not the experience, of trust, of warmth, of comfort. How can it be strong enough to move in a world founded on injustice? Is it truly humane to propose to human beings the dictum that their personalities "develop," that they become "richer" emotionally to the extent that they learn to trust, to open, to share, to eschew manipulation of others, to eschew agressive challenges to social conditions or mining these conditions for personal gain? Is it humane to form soft selves in a hard world?[1]

Sennett poses a tangled problem, and though he does not direct his questions specifically to Christians, they are questions which Christians must face. To begin to unravel the knot, I want to show how Christian faith makes some distinctions which Sennett does not.

It is true that Christian faith advocates trust, openness, sharing, nonmanipulation of others, and a way of life larger than personal gain. But these admonitions come with none of the sentimentality which Sennett imputes to the ideology of intimacy. On the contrary, while advocating openness and trust, Christian faith is also realistic about the factors which distort and prevent human intimacy. Christian faith claims that genuine intimacy is possible only as God mediates between us.

But Christian faith is subject to perversion, and in our day it is sometimes used to encourage the kind of personality Sennett writes about. Such a personality *is* unsuited to public life, and to the extent that the church contributes to this deformation of persons, the church undermines both the individual and public possibilities. So I want to look more closely at how faith confronts the problem of intimacy.

The ideology of intimacy is defined by three central tenets. One, that a human relationship of closeness and warmth, of depth and duration, is the most valuable—even the only valuable—experience that life affords. Two, that such a relation can be achieved by virtue of personal effort and will. Three, that only through such relationships can the individual personality develop to its fullest extent.

All three of these tenets are challenged by Christian faith. For Christian faith recognizes that we are alienated from one another, incapable (if left to our own devices) of genuine relationships. Our pride, our egos, our desire to control others or make them over in our own image—all these keep us from connecting with each other, except in the most self-interested ways. And how does Christian faith suggest that we deal with this problem and with the vast loneliness it brings? Certainly not by human means alone, since our strategies for closeness will be shaped by the very ego we need to overcome. No, we come close to each other not directly but through God's mediation in our lives. We find our deep unity with others not by seeking to embrace them, but by letting God embrace us. For it is in God's love that we find the bond between us; we find that bond by letting go of our own limited loves and receiving the unbounded love of the God who made us one.

The irony of the quest for intimacy is that it drives us apart. We try to cling to each other, and in clinging we distort the other person and ourselves through false dependencies, unreasonable expectations, unjustified hopes. With distortion our relations become strained, dishonest, and eventually self-destructive. But if we can approach each other through the God who is found at the deep center of our true selves, then we can come together not in distortion but in truth, not in self-interest but in compassion. When we allow God's love to mediate our relations, we place between us holy space, a space in which we can respect and be respected for who we are. In the spirit of that love, our relations do not depend on constant contact, on continual reassurance that we can somehow hold the weight of each other's lives. We can endure separation; we can disagree and argue and fight; we can, as we inevitably will, let each other down; and none of this frailty will destroy our relation if it is grounded in God's love rather than our egocentric image of what a relation should be.

Christian faith does not disavow intimate human relationships. It disavows that persons are capable of such relationships on their own. By putting God at the center of all relationships, Christianity opens the possibility of relations which are not close and warm yet can possess full value. The ideology of intimacy not only ends up destroying the intimacy it seeks; it also denies the value of nonintimate relations, of relations in public which lack depth, duration, intensity. Indeed, by definition, such relations are no relations at all, according to the norms of intimacy. To the extent that we are influenced by this understanding, we will spend our days cultivating the private and avoiding the public. But Christianity understands that the only authentic intimacy is with and through God, and in this intimacy the Christian is freed for a variety of relations in public, relations with the stranger, relations with persons whose needs and values are utterly alien to one's own. In the spacious hospitality of God's love, the Christian can become "intimate" even with people seen once, or not at all.

In God's hospitality we learn that close, warm, and enduring relations are not the only ones which enrich our lives. Indeed, we may learn less about ourselves in those relations than in more distant, occasional, and even abrasive ones; the person close to us may not have the perspective to see where we need to grow. So even if our main concern is self-development, the relations of strangers in public can be important to us.

But from the Christian viewpoint, self-development is not life's highest goal and greatest good. I do not say that Christianity denies self-development, as some of its gloomier interpreters have suggested. What those interpreters miss is the fact that our deepest and truest self is the life of God in us, that to seek God is to develop our own true selves. What Christian faith understands with intuitive certainty is the paradox of how we develop ourselves: "He who seeks his life shall lose it, while he who loses his life for my sake shall find it" (Matt. 10:34). Public life offers us the great and humanizing opportunity to abandon the self-serving search for self (which is bound to disappoint) and take up the service of others in all their "otherness." In that service we evoke that of God within us and meet Christ in the stranger. Only so shall we find ourselves.

3

If Christian faith does not support the ideology of intimacy, neither does it advocate the sort of public personality which Sennett seems to recommend. In the paragraph quoted earlier, he implies that the person best suited for public life is aggressive, untrusting, closed, possessive, manipulative, and out for personal gain: "Is it humane to form soft selves in a hard world?" he asks. And, in the name of humaneness, he implies that we should toughen ourselves against the onslaughts of public life.

But what is "humane" in this context? Sennett seems to be concerned that people with the "soft" virtues will be torn apart by public life, and I share that concern not only out of simple decency but because the fear of being racked and flayed keeps many Christians from ever entering the public realm. But is it humane to form hard selves in a hard world? No. Although the "tough" person may be able to protect self-interest, he or she extracts a high price from others. If we pursue Sennett's implication, we find a self-fulfilling prophecy: public life becomes more abrasive as we harden ourselves for it. The more we imagine the public to be an arena of combat and train people to be gladiators in it, the more combative and less compassionate the public life will be.

The world's logic is full of similar self-fulfilling prophecies. Fearing war, we prepare for the worst, thus increasing the likelihood that the worst will happen. Our schools, while holding up the vision of a cooperative society, train children to compete for rank and status, thus denying the vision an even chance. The Christian must see through this logic of self-defeat and refuse to participate in it. The vocation of the Christian is to break into such vicious circles with word of another prophecy—the good news that God has overcome our alienation and offers people the opportunity to become one and whole. This is the Christian's calling in public life: to witness to the possibility of compassion in a world of pain.

But Christian compassion differs from Sennett's "soft self" in two crucial ways. First, compassion is not offered in expectation that it will be returned. We know, through the life of Jesus, that love is not always met with love but is sometimes crucified instead. In Christ's compassion there is none of the naiveté which Sennett's image suggests, none of the wide-eyed surprise that public life can be difficult. The Christian is called to love in the midst of hate, and he or she knows that hate will sometimes seem to conquer. But the Christian also knows that things are not always as they seem, that God's grace continues to act in and through the most hateful situations.

Second, the Christian knows that crucifixion is followed by resurrection, that the way to true life always passes through some kind of death. There is no way to experience joy until one has known the depths of sorrow. There is no way to find a place to stand until one has fallen through. We will never see the light until we have known darkness. So Christian compassion grounds itself in the double paradox of love: our love will lead us into suffering, but that suffering will lead us into even greater love.

This paradox, of course, is a great mystery of faith, perhaps the most difficult of the mysteries for Christians to live out. Our "love" is so often based on pragmatic calculations (that it will bring about some desired result) or on romantic assumptions (that it will evoke love in return). As we learn that love does not work that way, as we begin to understand the dialectic of love, crucifixion, and resurrection, we often experience a failure of nerve. We retreat from those places where compassion is called for but where suffering lurks; we lack the faith that suffering will be overcome by love's power in us. And yet, the Christian witness stands or falls on this point. We are called to put our love in jeopardy so that love's victory can be demonstrated in our lives. As we are willing to lose our lives for Christ's sake, God's love flows through us to turn loss into gain, defeat into victory, death into life—for ourselves and others, too. But to experience the gain, the victory, the life, we must be willing to undergo the loss and the defeat and the death.

This is the faith of the "suffering servant," an image which tends to repulse people in our time. In an age of "assertiveness training" and "human potential," talk about suffering sounds a bit uncouth. Worse still, it is seen as pathological, a kind of masochism. So we need to remind ourselves that Christianity did not invent suffering but merely recognizes its reality in the world—a world so full of suffering that the real pathology is to live as if pain did not exist. Christ does not ask us to take on unnecessary pain but only to identify with the pain others feel. As we do so, we are led inevitably into the public realm.

So the Christian's response to Sennett's challenge is both simple and mysterious. "Is it humane to form soft selves in a hard world?" If by soft one means naive, no. But if one means compassionate, yes. In fact, it is more than "humane" to practice compassion in a hard world; it is divine. Only as we allow the world's pain to break us open to the flow of divine love will we be able to risk love in hard places. And only as we risk it will the private rhetoric of intimate caring become a public language of love.

4

I have, of course, been talking about "the way of the cross," a way as old as Christian faith itself. Being old, it is a way overlaid with images and understandings which contemporary men and women find difficult to understand, let alone adopt for themselves. It will never be an easy way to talk about—let alone to walk—but the church needs to find new ways in which to express its truth. In particular, since few of us will be called to lose our lives physically as Christ did on the cross, we need to find ways of seeing the cross in the lives we *are* called to lead. Otherwise our words about the cross will remain merely pious.

One clue lies in literally "seeing" the cross—I mean the physical object itself—with new eyes. Its very structure suggests its meaning. The arms reach up and down, symbolizing the ways we are torn between earthly and divine claims on our lives. The arms reach left and right, symbolizing the ways we are pulled between this and that loyalty in the world. In its very physical structure the cross is a symbol of the great contradictions of human experience, the tuggings and tearings of a thousand warring factors, and of the tension we feel as we stand in the middle of it all.

The cross which many Christians are called to bear involves the *contradictions* of contemporary life. And these contradictions are especially pronounced in the public realm. I want to indicate how Christian faith, the way of the cross, empowers us to live these contradictions creatively instead of retreating from them as we so often do. The way of the cross both leads us into public life and gives us the grace to live there.

We all know the contradictions of our own interior lives, that our actions often run counter to our ideals, that our weaknesses sometimes seem to cancel out our strengths, that when we are inspired to soar to altruistic heights we suddenly find weights of need and greed tied to our feet. We know also of "cosmic" contradictions, those awesome conundrums of existence which have bedeviled men and women for millennia. Why do the wicked flourish while good people suffer and die? How can there be so much evil if God is all-powerful and good?

Between the private and the cosmic lies the public realm. It, too, is riddled with contradictions, and these may be the most painful of all. Our inner contradictions can be hidden behind the walls of private life, behind the masks we wear. For many of us, those cosmic contradictions have been defined out of existence by a secularism which denies the presence of any benign power behind creation and reduces life to the play of random elements. But the contradictions of public life are visible to all, inevitable for anyone who enters the public sphere. Once in public, we cannot hide from its contradictions or define them away; perhaps that is why so many of us avoid the public realm to begin with.

Contradiction is the essence of public life. Here is the arena where a thousand warring factions assert their special interests, where it often seems impossible to find a single, common good. Here is the realm where compromise is the law of survival, a compromise which contradicts beliefs we deeply hold. In the public world our highest values often seem incompatible with one another; how, for example, can a society both grant freedom to all its members and assure equality for all? In public, the values we do manage to achieve are often contradicted by the unintended consequences of our actions: we lengthen human life through medical science only to increase the suffering and meaninglessness of old age among the beneficiaries. Or, we introduce progressive practices from one society into another only to find ourselves destroying the strength of the recipient society and increasing the misery of its people. In public life, contradictions abound, and when we enter it we will be pulled in a hundred different directions.

Psychologists tell us that much of our behavior is motivated by a desire to reduce tension. Wanting to live with a minimum of conflict, we devise ways to avoid these contradictions of the public realm. One way is to stay out of public altogether, to restrict our lives to the private sphere. This strategy does not rid our lives of public contradictions (for example, we may consume privately in ways that contribute to the deprivation of others) but in private our contradictions are less visible and we feel less accountable for them. Or, we reduce the tension of public life simply by abandoning those values and beliefs which create the tension to begin with. If we give up the idea that there is a common good (and many seem to have done so), then the public warfare of competing interests is no source of tension; the war will simply be won by whoever has the most power. If we yield up the conviction that a caring public is possible, then public cruelties will cause no sense of strain; we need only invoke the survival of the fittest. Perhaps Sennett's strong public person is such a survivor—a person who has chosen not to trust, not to share, not to be open, not to "eschew manipulation of others." Again, this posture does not rid our lives of contradictions. It merely dulls our awareness of them and the tension that such awareness brings.

5

The way of the cross challenges our natural tendency to avoid tension. The outreaching arms of the cross suggest the reality of tension, the poles of contradiction. But those same arms converge in the center, symbolizing Christian hope and experience that the contradictions can be transcended, overcome. The way of the cross challenges us not to remove tension from our lives by avoiding the places where tension is found, or by abandoning the convictions that cause us to feel tension. Instead, the cross points another way, a way of "living the contradictions," a way of taking tension into our lives and transforming it from a force of destruction into an energy of creation.

E. F. Schumacher has described this way in words I find evocative:

> . . . through all our lives we are faced with the task of reconciling opposites which, in logical thought, cannot be reconciled. . . . How can one reconcile the demands of freedom and discipline in education? Countless mothers and teachers, in fact, do it, but no one can write down a solution. They do it by bringing into the situation a force that belongs to a higher level where opposites are transcended —the power of love. . . . Divergent problems, as it were, force man to strain himself to a level above himself; they demand, and thus provoke the supply of, forces from a higher level, thus bringing love, beauty, goodness and truth into our lives. It is only with the help of these higher forces that the opposites can be reconciled in the living situation.[2]

Schumacher suggests that these higher powers, these powers of God's reconciliation, become available to us only as we place ourselves within the tension of opposites. If we spend our lives retreating from such places, if we live always in small, neat, and tidy rooms, then we will never be broken open to the play of great and life-giving forces within us. To enter the public life, with its chaos and confusions and constant contradictions, is to enter sometimes on paths of pain. But for that very reason, public life is a place where grace may abound.

There is a tendency toward "puristic" thinking among Christians, a tendency to want to resolve all dilemmas neatly, to draw back from situations which are ambiguous. We imagine, sometimes, that our faith requires us to lead tightly controlled lives, and this means placing ourselves only in those relationships which we can shape and form into some semblance of propriety. But by doing so, we deny God the opportunity to work miracles in our lives, to draw us beyond that which we think we can do. When we live lives of miniature and private scale for the sake of control, we deprive ourselves of the chance to have our tight and cramped inner space pulled open to the largeness and generosity which is life in the Spirit. We forget that we are not really in control and never can be, that God and God alone reigns over all of life, and that God's order is larger than our little logic will ever comprehend.

We want to live the logic of simple choices; give me this or give me that, but do not confuse me with the contradictions. Yet one of the basic movements of the Spirit in our lives, a movement on the way of the cross, is the movement from contradiction to paradox, from looking at life in terms of irreconcilable opposites to seeing that God's love embraces and unifies them all: "For everything there is a season, and a time for every matter under heaven: a time to be born, and a time to die; . . . a time to break down, and a time to build up; . . . a time to cast away stones, and a time to gather stones together . . ." (Eccles. 3:1–5). In the life of the Spirit, the irreconcilable poles of contradiction become the simultaneous truths of paradox. In the life of the Spirit we are empowered to live in the world of contradictions with a sense of the divine unity which lies behind it all.

Withdrawal from that world is not the message of Jesus' life. Jesus fully accepted life's contradictions and lived fully in the midst of them—in the power of love. They led him to the cross, and they will lead us there, too, for the cross is contradiction. But on the cross we discover the paradox that joy and the power for life lie on the other side of pain. The cross overcomes contradictions through the power of a God in whom all things are made one. That power will be ours only as we live fully amid the tension of our time. And that is the opportunity for growth and service afforded us by the public life.

7

Practicing the Public Life
The Congregation as Community

1

All through Scripture and long historical tradition, the church has been called to live as a gathered community of people who celebrate and support, challenge and resist, forgive and heal. God calls us to witness our inward sense of unity in outward ways; the life of the church and the experience people have within it are to manifest the oneness we find in the Spirit. When people look upon the church, it is not of first importance that they be instructed by our theology or altered by our ethics but that they be moved by the quality of our life together: "See how they love one another."

The call to community is constant, but the form the church community takes depends on how the church assesses its surroundings. Community tends to form in *reaction* to the larger society. Our image of community is, in microcosm, what we think the macrocosm should be but is not. The early church was a highly committed cadre for the succor and support of a minority persecuted by a hostile society. Under Constantine, Christianity received social sanction and support, and the church community became synonymous with the body politic. In the early middle ages, in the midst of cultural decline, the church took monastic form, becoming a community of withdrawal to preserve an endangered tradition.

To understand the church as community in our time, we must ask what image of the larger society animates us. The answer seems clear. We look upon our society as fragmented, disconnected, in process of disintegration, an arena in which human relations are often cold and competitive, sometimes violent. Neighborhood ties have been broken by individual mobility and urban sprawl. Relations in the work place have been depersonalized by bureaucracy. The family is in trouble, with parents forced to spend more time earning a living than raising children. Divorce, suicide, alcoholism —all the measures of personal and social disorder—are on the rise. More and more frequently we speak of our economy as being "out of control."

Clearly, that sketch is stark and overdrawn, more caricature than photograph. But it is, I think, the gross image of mass society against which the church forms itself as community in our time. Today, when clergy and lay people say they want "Christian community," they often mean they want the converse of mass society in every respect. Instead of conflict, the church should offer comfort; instead of distance between persons, intimacy; instead of criticism, affirmation and good will.

There is, of course, much good in these images of community, much that is vital to the nurture of the human spirit. But because the image of mass society is overdrawn, the communal reaction is overdrawn, too. The emphasis on intimate community as an antidote to mass society excludes some equally vital elements of human experience—elements which have much to do with our capacity for public life.

2

When we seek "community" as an escape from an impersonal society, we often think of community in familial terms. We imagine the church as a "parish family" in which intimacy is the primary and often exclusive goal; a family in which we can know and be known in depth, trust and be trusted without reservation. It is hard to argue against the family. But in the idealized image of family so popular in American culture, there is a threat to public life. For the family offers its members protections and privileges not available in the public realm. A church formed in that image of life together is not likely to prepare its members for full public involvement.

When an idealized image of family is imposed upon the church, our experience in the congregation becomes constricted. Now the church—where we might experience creative conflict, heterogeneity, and freedom for innovation—becomes dominated by the expectation of closeness and warmth.

Conflict, for example, tends to be devalued in the life of a "church family." As a result, church members receive little experience with problems of power and compromise and decision-making. Certainly conflict and power plays go on in church, but because intimacy is threatened by these realities, we cover them in hopes of maintaining a facade of peace. Our image of community forces people to hide their disagreements instead of getting them into the open where we might learn from them, where the problems might be worked through. Though such churches may achieve an apparent unity, it is fragile and unfulfilling, and behind it one often finds anger, frustration, and other taboo emotions.

When we envision the church as an idealized family, heterogeneity suffers as well. People with whom we cannot achieve intimacy, or with whom we do not want to be intimate, are squeezed out. Since intimacy often depends on social and economic similarities between people, our church communities become preserves for people of kindred class and status. Such a church does everything in its power to eliminate the strange and cultivate the familiar. Such a church can neither welcome the stranger nor allow the stranger in each of us to emerge. Such a church is a barrier to the public life.

In all of this there is irony and self-defeat. Our dislike of mass society and our desire to counter its trends lead us to construct communities of retreat rather than engagement, innovation, and change. Since engagement with the world around us will inevitably evoke diverse viewpoints and conflict among them, churches committed to a familial self-image forfeit their chance to become tools of collective action and become, instead, vehicles for emotive expression and relief. In this kind of community Christians fail to receive the training and empowerment which might enable them to confront the mass society and help to humanize it. Paralyzed by a fantasy image of the ideal church family, we are unable to invent new forms of church life which might minister to a public in need.

Ultimately, our hopes for intimate community have negative consequences for public life whether they succeed or fail. If they succeed, it is often because of a strong ideology or the presence of a powerful mother/father figure around whom everything revolves. In those cases, the community easily becomes self-contained; it can be joined only by those who conform to the ideology or accept the authority of the leader; it draws some people in too deep, excludes many others, and cannot serve a public function.

But even more likely, attempts at intimate community will fail. People come together only to find that they are inwardly blocked from sharing at the deep levels they had hoped for. Or, having shared, they experience inadequate response or even betrayal. Burdened with a fantasy of community which is not fulfilled by experience, they give up on community altogether, returning their energies to the inner circles of family life and self. Succeeding or failing, the fantasy of intimate community is inimical to public life.

We need to redefine the church community, not against the backdrop of mass society but toward the promise of public life. As we do so, we will begin to envision communities which are not mere extensions of private security, but which bridge the private and the public, leading us from the familiarities of private life into the strangeness of the public realm. In this way, the church can become a "halfway house," moving people from fear of the world around them into a role as cocreators of a world which is both God's and their own.

3

The idea of community is vital even if we have misconstrued it. We must not abandon the quest. It is the equation between community and familial intimacy which we must abandon. More to the point, we must abandon our idealized image of the family in the light of Christian realism.

The call to become a family is often couched in the exhortation that we become "brothers and sisters again." We could save ourselves from self-defeating sentimentality merely by remembering what *real* brothers and sisters are like, for they make war on each other at least as often as they coexist in peace! If we would look at the family with open and unromantic eyes, we would see that it contains its own versions of much that pains us about the public life. We would see that there is no place to hide from the problems of human coexistence, and we would be less likely to make a fetish of the family, a fantasy of community, and a spectre of the public realm.

Like the public, every family must deal with problems of power. Family members contend for power for the same reasons which motivate members of the public—resources are scarce and conflict follows. In fact, the family provides some of the most telling illustrations of our tendency to take abundant nonmaterial goods and treat them as if they were scarce. How many times have children felt that parental love was unevenly distributed, that the more my brother or sister gets, the less there is for me? Even the social distance we experience in public, the gap between strangers, has its analogs in family life. Anyone who has raised a teenager knows that a fourteen- and a forty-year-old simply live in different worlds! Though they are of one flesh and one blood, they are strangers to each other. Deeper still, family life often presses us to points where we encounter the strange and the unknown in ourselves or our mate, a fact well-known by couples weathering the storms of "midlife crises."

The apostles of intimacy may insist that a true marriage, a true family, would rid itself of all this strife, but such advice is a snare and a delusion. A true marriage will not simply experience conflict and "hang on" in and through it; a true marriage will turn these problems into occasions for more profound knowledge of self, of other, of God. The task in marriage, as in all human relations, is not to perfect or abandon it, but to let its conflicts and contradictions pull us open to larger truth. Christianity understands all our relations—even the closest ones—to be broken and imperfect, but forgiven and redeemed. Christians are called to live in recognition of both realities.

If we would reread the Scripture with open eyes, we would see that it does not idealize the family. The story of the prodigal son, to take one example, teaches some of the hardest lessons of family life (and of the nature of God's love). And some of Jesus' hardest sayings have to do with family: "If anyone comes to me and does not hate his own father and mother and wife and children and brothers and sisters . . . he cannot be my disciple" (Luke 14:26). Surely Jesus' own family was filled with tensions. Recall the episode where Jesus is teaching; his mother and brothers arrive asking to see him. "And he replied, 'Who are my mother and my brothers?' And looking around on those who sat about him, he said, 'Here are my mother and my brothers! Whoever does the will of God is my brother, and sister, and mother' " (Mark 3:33—35).

Like most of Jesus' teachings, his words on family are a two-edged sword, having the quality of paradox. For while they clearly indicate that the nuclear family is not the Christian's highest loyalty, they also suggest that the kingdom will come in family form. What a profound challenge this paradox poses to our conventional thinking about "family"! The kingdom will come when we can regard all of those strangers as our brothers and sisters; when we can embrace all of the contradictions and conflicts of public life with familial compassion; when we know that under the father/motherhood of God we, all of us, in our astonishing variety, are made as one. That is a great vision. But until we can abandon our idealized vision of family and let that word embrace far more than it normally does, we will only domesticate the church and the kingdom by conceiving them in familial terms.

4

Is there an image for the church community which includes the sense of family but also helps us make sense of conflict and diversity—an image which will allow community to "educate" us (that is, lead us out) into the public realm? I have been helped by thinking of the church as "a school of the Spirit," a place where God is continually drawing me out of myself into the larger life. A good school has familial features, an ethos of caring for its students. But a school will also correct and upbraid and uproot us, introduce us to the strange and unfamiliar, teach us a truth larger than our own.

Our idealized images of community will always fail us, always be given the lie by experience, and for good theological reason: those images are idolatrous. They project upon community such needs for personal nurture and support as can only be met by our relation to God. By idealizing community, we invest in it those trusts and loyalties which belong to God alone. Small wonder that community so conceived has so often failed. But if we can see community as a school of the Spirit, we can learn from our idolatry and its failures.

I know the importance of being open to such learning, having lived now for six years in a residential community of some seventy people who share a daily round of worship, physical work, study, decision-making, and caring for one another. There is laughter and joy in this community, but there is also pain—the pain of letting one another down, the pain of being seen for what one really is rather than what one would like to be, the pain of conflict with persons we may someday learn to love but will probably never like. Community, as I know it, is a continual process of unmasking, of having to let go of illusions about ourselves and others. How can we keep these disillusionments from producing defeat and despair, from driving us out of community life? Only by receiving them for what they are—nudgings of the Spirit, holy teachings, intended to show us where the power of life really lies; only by receiving our experience in community as schooling in the Spirit.

Once, during a particularly trying time of my life in community, I came up with a definition which still seems true: "Community is that place where the person you least want to live with always lives!" Later, I developed a corollary: "And when that person moves away, someone else arises to take his or her place!" I am only half-joking, for the stress and tension which lie behind those jests are inevitable in our life together. If we cannot learn to value such experience, we will abandon community. And why value it? Because such experience reveals the truth about ourselves and others, the truth about our need for God. Only by being schooled in such truth will we be able to live together.

Community always contains the person you least want to live with because there will always be someone who draws out the quality you least like in yourself. The external stranger reminds us of the inner stranger whom we do not want to acknowledge or confront. It is a painful experience, but only as this darkness is "educated" out of us will we be prepared for life together. Such pain is not a denial of community; it is a fulfillment of the role that community can play in our lives, the role of drawing us out into the common life.

If the church could become such a community—a place where people confront the stranger in each other and in themselves, and still know that they are members one of another—it would help people enter the public sphere. But critics have long claimed that the typical congregation contains no strangeness, that it is a bland and homogeneous blend. And earlier on, I myself argued that the emphasis on intimacy has created congregations which are drawn from single layers of our stratified society. If these claims are true, the congregation would seem to be the last place for an experiment in living with diversity.

Deeper probes will reveal that the congregation's uniformity is only apparent, maintained for the sake of image. Behind the facade of the typical white, middle-class congregation there lurks considerable variety in taste, opinion, viewpoint, conviction. But that variety has been suppressed for a fiction, the illusion that the church must be a family at play, avoiding conflict at all costs. It is a costly illusion. Some people have been driven from the church by boredom and unreality, while some who have stayed are filled with silent resentment over conflicts they are unable to express. Behind the polite and placid exterior of many congregations one finds a sad misuse of emotional energy. If the energy given to cover conflict could be channeled to creative use, the church would be a livelier place, a place at once more human and more divine.

Not only would the church be livelier, it would also exemplify the quality most vital to the renewal of public life—the capacity of a common commitment to hold us together despite diversity and conflict. In a society like ours, with its fear of isolation and its quest for intimacy, relationships often take one of three forms: intimacy in which conflict is suppressed, indifference and the absence of contact, or hostility in which no positive potentials are presumed. What is missing are the relations of strangers who will never achieve intimacy, but who meet with a sense of commonality which makes creative conflict possible—meetings of the sort which characterize the healthy public life. Can the church learn to model that mode of relationship?

The faith in which the church is grounded emerges from a story of conflict. Never in the biblical record is that conflict finally resolved, never are we delivered into a utopia of perfect harmony. Even the first disciples and the members of the early church, even those beleaguered minorities who had every reason to stick together, even they were fractured by dissent. But in the Christian story, conflict is the context in which the faith is taught, the text on which the lesson builds. In the midst of conflict moves God the teacher, offering the gift of reconciliation even when it is refused over and over again. As a biblical people, we should welcome conflict as an opportunity to learn that our wholeness lies in the one who sustains us all.

5

How can a congregation turn conflict from a destructive event into an occasion for schooling in the Spirit? Out of many possibilities I want to focus on decision-making within the congregation. Conflict most often emerges in the church (and in public) when a diverse group must decide on a common course of action. How can we make such decisions in a spirit which seeks the unity beyond our differences?

The church could take a step in that direction by trying to make decisions as an act of worship. Normally, we think of worship and decision-making as two quite different activities—the one sacred, the other secular; the one quiet and harmonious, the other noisy and contentious. But, at bottom, both involve the same quest for truth. If we can focus on the truth which unites us rather than the opinions which divide, we will stand a better chance of learning the redemptive power of conflict. Of course, everyone thinks his or her opinions *are* truth, so we cannot resolve the matter merely by playing with words. But if we approached decision-making as a worshipful quest for truth, we would put our differences in a context where they become helps, not hindrances.

Those congregations which have liturgical worship might develop a liturgy for decision-making. In such a ritual, we would be reminded of the common faith in which our conflict occurs; we would seek to approach the decision in the open, attentive, and receptive manner of prayer; we would be invited to recall times when our own opinions proved aggressively wrong-headed; we would pray together for forgiveness of our biases and the grace to understand each other's points of view. In the midst of such a liturgy, it would also be important to call for periods of silent meditation as the decision was being made. So often we heighten our conflicts by trying to "talk them out," only to end up in a warfare of words. Where words divide us, silence can unite us, for in that silence people can sort and sift their passions and be given opportunities to hear beyond the words. In my own community's business meetings we sometimes say that the longer and the more loaded the agenda before us, the longer should be our periods of silent worship, and results often prove the rightness of this approach.

The community in which I live is grounded in Quaker faith and practice, so we try to make our decisions by "the sense of the meeting" rather than by majority vote. I want to suggest this method (popularly known as "consensus") as a way of decision-making which evokes the constructive side of conflict, for it compels us to do the one thing essential to the public life—seek the unity beneath our differences.

Consensus means that no decision is made until everyone in the group is willing to go along with it. That definition alone is enough to terrify people who have no experience of the method, for it sounds time-consuming, laborious, and ultimately impossible. How much more efficient to line up the votes and count the winning side! But such objections to consensus are rooted in an assumption that the church must make decisions, no matter what the cost; that somehow "decisions" are products which the church must turn out. Again, I suggest the image of the church as a "school of the Spirit." Consensus may result in fewer decisions more slowly taken, but in the process people will learn more about themselves, each other, and the God in our midst than is possible when a decision, not spiritual growth, is the goal.

Consensus is not as efficient as voting, to be sure (though I wonder if anyone has ever calculated the time and effort required when a majority decision leaves an agitated minority to be placated or disarmed). But consensus drives us to a deeper place in ourselves and our relationships than voting ever can. Where voting calls us to defend our own position and defeat others, consensus calls us to scrutinize our own views and listen to others with care. Where voting results in a majority overpowering a minority, consensus teaches us what it means to be a member of a body which must act together or not at all. Consensus cultivates the virtues required for the public life.

What is it about consensus which compels these changes in attitude and behavior, which forces us to deal creatively with conflict? Primarily this: when a group cannot make a decision until everyone is willing to go along, the tenor of the discussion is quite different than when the majority rules. Now, instead of looking for our differences, instead of looking for weaknesses in each other's arguments which we can rebut, we look instead for similarities, for strengths, for common ground. When the majority rules we try to sharpen the disagreements between us to force people to choose a side. When decisions are made by consensus we seek a synthesis which brings the opposites together. Consensus does not deny or ignore conflict, but uses it for creative purposes. Here, the tension produced by two truths in conflict does not tear us apart but presses us to find a "third truth," one deeper and more embracing than anything the adversaries had imagined.

At the same time, consensus protects the individual's right to conscience (as must the public life). If even one person has grave doubts about the morality of an action, the group operating by consensus cannot move. This may sound like organizational insanity, since all of us have been in voting situations where a few people have remained obstinantly unconvinced of the majority's wisdom. But under consensus the individual who objects will tend to do so on carefully considered grounds; when persons are given the power and trust which consensus bestows, they tend to filter out their minor differences and stand against the group only when they must. Consensus requires not only that we listen carefully to one another, but also that we listen carefully to our own inner truth. If that truth is persistent, consensus gives us the chance to demonstrate that truth is not a matter of numbers.

People often ask whether consensus decision-making, for all its spiritual virtues, is not a practical impossibility, an unaffordable luxury, in a large church. How do you reach consensus with five hundred people, let alone a couple of thousand? So long as a large church tries to operate as a whole on all important matters, it will not only be unable to make decisions by consensus, it will be unable to do a great number of things conducive to its members' spiritual growth. The first need in a large congregation is to subdivide into human-scale units (house churches, or covenant groups, or "base communities") where persons can hear and be heard. Such groups as these can practice consensus decision-making, and when the time comes for the whole body to make a decision together, the experience people have had in these smaller groups will facilitate the process.

Of course, most public decisions are made by majority vote, so one may wonder whether consensus decision-making really prepares people for public life. Consensus teaches a new way of looking for the unity which lies beneath our differences, a way of using our differences not as weapons but as springboards toward new truth. The public life badly needs people with this capacity, people who can use that insight and that experience even in adversary situations. If a church could make even a few decisions by consensus, it would help raise up such leaders for the public realm.

6

I have argued that the church, picturing itself as a close and warm family, tends to suppress conflict, depriving its members of a vital lesson in public life. That same familial image undermines the public life in another way—by excluding the stranger from its midst. If the church is to serve as a school of the Spirit, and as a bridge between the private and the public realms, it must find ways of extending hospitality to the stranger. I do not mean coffee hours designed to recruit new members for the church, for these are aimed at making the stranger "one of us." The essence of hospitality—and of the public life—is that we let our differences, our mutual strangeness, be as they are, while still acknowledging the unity that lies beneath them.

Openness to the stranger, and to letting the stranger be, is resisted by the basic dynamics of community formation. An intimate community is formed by an act of exclusion—"we" are in and "they" are out. The very fact that a group of people have a sense of community with one another suggests that they have drawn a boundary around themselves, that they see themselves as different from the surrounding world. The stranger threatens the foundations of such a community by blurring the boundary; the stranger must either be kept out or made to become like us.

If a community is to open itself to the stranger, it must come to terms with its own need to be different, to be set apart. It is a basic impulse in human life, this need to distinguish ourselves from others, and it begins not in community but in the individual. At its best, this is the impulse toward individuation, toward integrity: we need this sense of self to avoid being shaped by whatever powers happen to be playing upon us at the time. But at its worst, the need to be different is the source of racism and sexism and ethnocentrism: we distinguish ourselves by putting down someone else, and the natural differences between people become invidious rather than cause for celebration.

The irony is that every community which rejects the stranger and anxiously protects "its own kind" gives witness, not to the strength of its identity, but to its deep-rooted insecurity. When a community's identity is rooted in the truth that we are all members of one another—that our deepest identity is in our commonality in God—then it can embrace the stranger with grace and ease. But a community which is uncertain about its true name will be unable to accept the challenge which the stranger represents. We can be receptive to all manner and condition of women and men only by knowing that our common name is in the God who made us all and made us one.

If the church could live in that faith, its opportunities for hospitality to the stranger would be endless. I recently spent several days at a soup kitchen run by Christians in one of the poorest parts of New York City. Each day, a simple meal of soup and bread and tea is served to the strangers who come in off the street—men and women whose lives have been wasted by mental illness, alcohol, drugs, poverty; people barely able to survive. Those who come in to eat are not asked to give anything in return, but only to receive a gift of food. But those who serve, as I did those few days, receive a gift as well, a gift of understanding. There I was, standing among people whose neighborhood I seldom enter and who never enter mine, people I would have crossed the street to avoid. As I stood there it came to me that if fear were called for, they should be afraid of me, for I represent and profit by a society which has left them bereft.

In this soup kitchen, this place of hospitality, I was able to see the connections between myself and these strangers. I felt the unity which runs beneath our vast and tragic differences. I was reminded that we are members one of another, members of the public. And I thought how helpful it would be if more churches had more ministries like this, not only for the sake of those who are hungry, but for the sake of those who need to be reminded of their connections and accountability to the least of these, our brethren.

Here is a possibility of quite a different kind: the church could extend hospitality to strangers by offering to host dialogues between groups in the community who are, or may be, in conflict. I mean such groups as teachers and school boards, teenagers and police, blacks and whites in "changing neighborhoods," labor and management, "gays" and "straights." Everywhere we look today there are groups lining up against one another, viewing each other with all the fear and hostility that the stranger can evoke. The church might help such groups achieve, not family, but mutual respect, the capacity to see each other as strangers who are members of one another.

Of course, the church can offer hospitable space to strangers only as it provides such space for its own members. If a congregation is suppressing conflict in its own life, it will find the stranger too threatening. When the stranger enters a church, he or she must feel that here is a place where people know their true name, a place where people face conflict without flying apart, where difference does not lead to judgment, where diversity does not breed distrust.

7

How can the congregation become such a place? Not by first seeking closeness and warmth with each other but by letting God stand in its midst as the one who offers hospitality, the one who mediates conflict, the one in whom we find the truth which unites. If such a God is a mere idea for us and not a living experience, consensus will not work; we will constantly try to manipulate the outcome rather than letting ourselves be led. If we do not know the reality of God, we will never welcome the stranger but will respond instead with defensiveness and fear. The church will practice the public life not simply by proper programming, not simply by right belief. The church will practice the public life by practicing the living presence of God, a presence in which gaps are bridged, wounds healed, obstacles surmounted, the many made one.

In my own community we spend much time dealing face-to-face with the fears and conflicts which arise among us, trying to "work things out." We talk and we listen and we try to understand; we reorganize our routines, trying to find structural solutions for our dilemmas. Sometimes we succeed, but only for a while. Then new difficulties occur and we have to summon the energy to deal with each other once again. It is a wearying process and I am convinced we would give it up were it not for one constant of our life together —the daily meeting for worship.

Each morning we gather for thirty or forty minutes of silent meditation and prayer. In that silence we often experience a healing which comes not from our own flawed wisdom but from the movement of God's Spirit in our midst. In the silence, as each of us centers on the light of God within us, one can sometimes feel the anger and anxiety subsiding as love and peace rise among us. Sometimes, people will speak out of the silence, but when they speak it seems to come from a source deeper and truer than the one on which we draw when we are actively trying to "work things out." The voices one hears in meeting for worship are voices of healing, not division, of vulnerability, not self protection, voices we can speak only as we practice the presence of God.

Recently I visited a Trappist monastery where I was reminded of what it might mean for a community to center its life on that presence. Here, seventy men maintain a discipline designed to focus their attention on God rather than directly on one another. They live in silence much of the time (using sign language when it is necessary) so that their whole life can have the quality of prayer. They worship together not once but seven times a day, allowing the liturgy and the sacraments to represent God's love in their midst. When one of them has a problem with another, he takes it to the Abbot, a man richly endowed with the gift of spiritual guidance, the ability to illumine conflict with the light of divine love. In every way, these monks live a life which discourages direct encounter between them in favor of the individual encounter with God.

I had as little "interaction" with the monks as they have with each other. Yet never have I felt a stronger sense of community. Never have I been in a place where people had more compassion for each other—and for the stranger in their midst. While I was there I felt the nurture and support of their prayers, and I feel it even now. For me it is compelling evidence that true community arises not from our own social graces but from the mediation of God's grace among us.

I do not suggest that the congregation should become a monastery, but only that we find ways of adapting this key insight of monastic life. By way of illustration, think of those moments in church life when people turn to one another for counsel and support on personal problems. To let God mediate our relationships means, in this case, that when one listens to another's need, one listens not with a sense of personal power to "straighten things out" but with a sense of God's presence which alone can heal. If we can do that, we will not carry the impossible burden of trying to "solve" each other's problems, a burden which first creates guilt over one's own inadequacy and then resentment over the other's expectations. Freed from the need to "solve" anyone's problem, we can be fully present to each other as friends, embodiments of the love God has for each of us in our need.

Or take those moments of conflict when people disagree over some issue which has arisen in the church. If our relationships are rooted in mere compatability, our differences will drive us apart. But if our relations are grounded in the God who made us individual but one, the God who calls us all to search for truth, then we can maintain our bonds despite persistent differences—for both truth and our own integrity depend on our ability to speak in love a word the other may not wish to hear.

Or, to illustrate once more, when we encounter strangers on the world's normal terms, we meet with suspicion and distrust, alert for the signals which will warn us to throw up barriers, or flee. But when we meet in a setting where God is host between us, we meet with new possibilities in mind. Who is this stranger whom God has sent our way? What chance is God now giving us to learn something new? What opportunity are we being offered to serve and be served? When we allow God to be the third person in all our meetings, fear is replaced by hope, and hope fulfills itself.

The church can become a community which frees us from the fears that breed private seclusion and leads us instead toward the creative possibilities of public life. If this is to happen, it will depend not so much on the sociological sophistication of church programs as on the quality of the congregation's spiritual life. For only as we learn to discern the presence of God—within us, between us, among us, beyond us—will we develop human relations full of hope and healing, relations of the sort which could renew our public life.

8

Building the Public Life
The Congregation in Mission

1

Christian faith is marked by its emphasis on incarnation, on the embodiment of truth. Whatever truth the church possesses is not to remain abstract but is to be lived by those who believe. The good news Christians are given is meant to be enacted in our corporate and individual lives, not only in the church but also in the world.

Having explored the idea of the public and its implications, having looked at how the church might preach a public theology and practice a public psychology, I turn now to the church's mission in the world beyond its walls. What can the church do to help provide public experience for an essentially private people? How can Christians help the public invent itself, discover itself, empower itself, become itself?

As I have insisted from the beginning, my concern is not merely for the *idea* of the public but for the dynamic, daily *experience* of public life. The idea may open the experience to us, but then we need the experience to validate the idea. In part we need to help people interpret the experience they already have in public terms. In part we need to help people have new and more compelling forms of public experience.

Both of these tasks involve "creating public space." By that I mean not only physical space in which strangers can interact, space which is more hospitable toward public life than the space found in most of our cities; I refer also to symbolic space and institutional space. As I hope to show, we can give strangers space to interact by sharing symbols of the common life in the public realm, and by designing institutions which bring strangers together in new and creative ways. In all of this the church can perform a ministry of incarnation, helping the word "public" take on living flesh.

2

I begin at the heart of the congregation's life, with the act of worship. To be more precise, I mean "public worship," for corporate praise of God is meant to be a public, not a private act. The idea of the public is driven deep into the history and language of worship, as witness the root meaning of the word "liturgy":

> Liturgy is, in the original and classical sense of the word . . . a "public work," a contribution made by a free citizen of the *polis* to the celebration and manifestation of the visible life of the *polis*.[1]

Clearly, the church in our time has lost the sense of public worship. Today, our worship is public only in the sense that anyone may enter the sanctuary on Sunday morning and join with us—and there are churches where the "right" to worship is proscribed by barriers of race or class. This limited sense of public worship is diminished even further by the fact that it occurs in a "sanctuary," a place removed from the world, apart from the settings where public life is lived. When we praise God only in private, there is little chance that our worship will help the public become visible to itself.

The church could help build a public by worshiping in public places. If a public is to discover and sustain itself, our deepest symbols of unity, of brokenness, and of longing for reconciliation must be shared. That is the nature of worship—a symbolic celebration of the unity we have, a petition for forgiveness of the ways we have broken our bond, and a receptivity to the wholeness that is promised by God. When we hold such rites only in private we strip the public realm of the symbols needed to evoke a public, and we remove ourselves from the realities of the public world in which the reconciliation of strangers must occur.

Any suggestion that religious symbols should play a public role is likely to be met with stern reminders that our society is founded on a separation of church and state. But since—as we have seen—the public realm consists of much more than the state, this wall of separation need not be construed as a barrier to public religion. Yet this is precisely what we have done. Not only have we banished religious symbolism from the public realm; we have allowed that realm to be occupied, even overwhelmed, by the symbols of consumerism, symbols not of God but of mammon—buying and selling, having and owning, consuming and competing for more. Is it any wonder that the "public" which forms around such symbols as these is involved in little more than the regulation of conflicting self-interests, is incapable of projecting visions of a common good? In a society which strips its public life of religious images and meanings, and allows the vacuum to be filled largely by commercialism, the only stimulants to imagining new worlds are in the private realm. It is no wonder that the new worlds we imagine are essentially private and even narcissistic.

The church can help renew our public life by making itself more visible in the public sphere. Public space is available to us. Do we have the imagination to use that space to pronounce the promise of unity and the healing of wounds? If we were to do so we would not be inventing radical new practices but reclaiming ancient traditions. I think, for example, of the great festival-day parades so characteristic of Catholic or Orthodox societies, parades which revivify people's sense of belonging to one another. But these examples raise a question: is public worship possible, or even legitimate, only in societies which are more homogeneous than ours? In our pluralistic nation, how can Christians worship publicly without giving offense to Jews, Muslims, atheists, and all the others who make up the American population?

That question goes to the heart of the discomfort, even squeamishness, we feel about worshiping in public. And our response reveals the disastrous conclusion which Americans have drawn from pluralism—that diversity requires religion to retreat into private, to withdraw from the public realm. We fail to recognize that a pluralistic society is weakened, not strengthened, when we remove religious meanings from public experience, for such a society then loses the possibility of significant coherence. The key to the maintenance of a healthy pluralism is continual dialogue between religious traditions, continual efforts to express our own integrity and discover what we share in common. When we remove faith from public discourse, the dialogue stops, and society is forced to find its common ground elsewhere. The ground it finds may be common, but it will necessarily be lower ground than that provided by the great religious traditions. The public expression of great religious truths gives us our best chance to find the framework of love and justice within which true pluralism can thrive.

Perhaps our problem goes deeper still. Perhaps we resist true public worship because worship in private allows us to emphasize that which makes us different, that which divides us, rather than that which unites. In private, in the company of "our own kind," we can laud our uniqueness and even denigrate others without being checked against reality, without being called to account. But public expression is accountable. Under the pressure of accountability religious discourse may be forced to reach for the essentials which unite us.

How can the church "go public" with its worship? There are some simple possibilities. Each summer, the Protestant churches in the town where I was raised held a joint service so large that it required the use of an open amphitheatre in the middle of a busy park. The purpose in being there was to gain space, not to make a public witness. But I still recall the impact of those services when, with strangers passing by—some oblivious to us, some pausing to watch, others joining in—I felt a heightened sense of the power and meaning of worship, of the connection between words of faith and the broken world.

More recently, members of my community took a three day retreat at a seashore motel where, each morning, we worshiped on a beachside patio with sunbathers and beachcombers all around. On our last day the motel manager bid us farewell, saying how touched he had been by our group and its daily worship and his sense of "how much you love one another." The manager was Jewish, the group was Christian, yet something basic and common had been communicated by our public worship. And surely the manager had no knowledge of how closely his words followed the accolade given the early church as reported by Tertullian.

Even if you have not had experiences such as these, recall public caroling at Christmastime and the warm sense of community which grows between those who sing and those who listen.

In all of these instances, the classical meaning of "liturgy" begins to be fulfilled. Here is worship as a "public work," worship helping to create a public. Here is a "celebration and manifestation of the visible life" of the community. If the spirit of such worship is narrow, exclusive, and judgmental, it will soon be ignored or refuted. But if it is open and expansive, inviting men and women to declare their deepest connection with one another, then it will be received as a contribution to the common life.

The possibilities are endless. A church could do something as simple as processing into the sanctuary and recessing from it along a route that takes people out-of-doors, down the public streets. People can hold services in their yards, visible to their neighbors. Choirs can present programs of sacred music on the courthouse square. Religious art can be displayed along the corridors of shopping malls. Public preaching could be revived in city parks, or entire services could be held in parks and city squares. Or why not a whole new style of church architecture with plenty of glass on the ground level so that a congregation at worship would be visible to passersby? Any situation, looked at long enough and with an ample imagination, will reveal ways for the church at worship to enter the public realm and help renew the public life.

3

Not every action the church takes in the public realm need be overtly "religious." Any act which helps people recall their commonality is religious in the sense of helping to "rebind" our life together. I want to look now at some forms of church mission to the public which do not involve explicit religious symbols or ceremonies.

One arena for action, one place where a public might be gathered, is in the shopping mall. The mall—as I have already suggested—is a dubious development because it puts private boundaries around the space where people come to shop, a space which historically, in the form of village markets and city streets, has been public property. In the process, malls have drawn the public and its attention away from the streets, making them less attractive and more dangerous than they once were. Still, the mall is one of the primary places where strangers can meet, so we must discover how the mall might be reclaimed for public purposes.

If we could do so, we would recapture the original insight behind the mall. Victor Gruen, the architect who conceived the idea and designed some of the first models in America, spoke often of how the contemporary mall had failed to fulfill his hopes:

> His original purpose . . . was for centers that would be "more than just selling machines." They were to include medical offices, rooms for club activities, circulating libraries and post offices in addition to shops. He wanted them closely related to nearby housing—spots of urbanity in the long suburban stretches.[2]

> . . . Gruen wrote that malls "can provide the need, place and opportunity for participation in modern community life that the ancient Greek Agora, the medieval market place, and our own town squares provided in the past."[3]

Clearly, the man who originated malls saw them as centers for the public life in communities built around private needs and interests. But in the hands of "fast-buck promoters and speculators," said Gruen, the mall became dedicated to turning a profit at the expense of building a community. Unlike the city streets, where commercial activity and public experience have always overlapped (thus proving that the two are not necessarily opposed) the mall is dedicated to private consumption and profit in ways that often exclude the public; witness the ban on leafletting or picketing in most malls. Since the mall is one of the few places where strangers gather in large numbers, its restrictiveness is especially damaging to our chances for a public life.

What actions might be taken to liberate public space within the shopping mall? Again, the possibilities seem endless, limited only by our imaginations. For example, a group of voluntary associations might band together to rent meeting space in the mall. Though mall space is prohibitively expensive for most nonprofit groups, several groups sharing the cost might find it affordable. The simple presence of a storefront with the names of these organizations would remind passersby of the concerns of the larger public to which we all belong. The presence of these groups would draw some people to the mall for public rather than private reasons, thus giving the mall a new identity. People who came to the mall simply to shop might find themselves intrigued, or in need of the help these organizations offer, or wanting to volunteer for one or another of these causes. If more voluntary associations would conduct their business in the malls, they would serve as magnets around which a public might collect.

Another possibility involves the "market research" one sometimes finds in malls. In many shopping centers, interviewers with clipboards and questionnaires are continually asking shoppers to sample a new candy or help name a new deodorant so that manufacturers can be responsive to "public opinion." There is no reason the same approach could not be used to build public opinion in the deeper sense. Shoppers could be asked to comment on issues facing the community, thus stimulating individual reflection and expression. Their answers could be tallied in some central and visible place so that the community could see its own reflection in a statistical mirror. I imagine, for example, some sort of electronic scoreboard featuring an "issue of the day," reminding people as they pursue private interests that they also share a common life.

Or, I can envision some sort of "public forum" located in an open space in the center of the mall. Here speakers (live or on videotape) would present brief but pointed arguments on an issue, and the audience could either listen and be informed or be given a chance to react. The mall is the most logical place for the American version of Hyde Park's Corner, and as we develop such structures for the sharing and sharpening of viewpoints and convictions, we help to renew the public life.

Another illustration, of quite a different sort: what if there were a booth or kiosk in the middle of the mall which functioned as a "switchboard" for matching human resources with human problems, or simply for bringing together people with common interests? A bulletin board would do the trick, but with a volunteer staff and a system of files and indexes the possibilities for linking people —for building a public—would be richer and more complex. Here is the place to leave your name and number if you have household jobs which youngsters might do; here is the place to come if you are a teenager looking for hourly work. Or suppose you want to learn some basics about auto repair; come to the switchboard to find the names of people who have offered to share their knowledge with others. Perhaps you are trying to start a group interested in raising tropical fish or discussing the situation in China; the switchboard is the place to look for potential members. A simple device such as this helps recover human connectedness in a fragmented society, and in the process helps renew our sense of belonging to one another in the public life.

The illustrations could go on and on. There are myriad ways of liberating mall space from its private captivity and opening it to public use. The barriers to this sort of action lie not in the tendencies of mall management to protect their "turf," nor even in the problem of high rentals. Both of these can be overcome by the concerted action of community groups, for a good mall manager does not want to alienate the major institutions or leaders of the community. The barrier to such action lies within ourselves. When we think of "going public" in these ways, we experience feelings of hesitancy and embarrassment. In our private culture such things "just aren't done."

To overcome this inner barrier, the support and encouragement of a group is essential. Actions such as these will be taken only when the congregation understands their significance and only when the individuals who might undertake them feel strong collective support. Private life feels safe and public life feels risky, but a congregation which provides affirmation and assurance can help people take the risk of leading public lives.

4

If the public life is to be renewed, some of our action must take place on the public streets. Although malls have taken over many commercial functions, the streets are still the sinews and arteries of our communities. They can and must be reclaimed for public purposes. Though malls may open themselves to a balanced, educational presentation of conflicting points of view, they will not soon permit the passionate expression of one side of an issue. Such expression has occurred historically on the public streets, and has been especially vital to oppressed and powerless minorities in making their claims upon the public. Where the minority cannot be heard, we all suffer, for under those circumstances there is no public, only a state on its way toward totalitarianism.

The importance of street action is nowhere better illustrated than in the recent history of the black civil rights struggle. During the sixties, America took long-overdue steps toward establishing equality in opportunities for education, employment, housing, and voting itself. But the seventies saw a slowdown in this movement toward justice, and even some reversals. Is it only coincidental that street demonstrations were a major tactic of the sixties, but were abandoned in favor of conventional politics and backstage bargaining in the seventies? Is it mere coincidence that progress towards equal rights slowed as the struggle left the streets?

The demonstrations of a decade ago served at least two purposes. First, they raised the awareness of white Americans that something was wrong, something which could no longer be ignored. Whether one was sympathetic with the marchers or hostile to them, one was related to the issue, one felt part of a public struggle. Second, the street actions helped form an empowering sense of community among blacks and their allies. This sense of collective strength gave an oppressed people faith that their bondage could be broken. In both of these respects, street demonstrations played a powerful role in shaping an American public. Blacks became empowered to claim their public rights, and whites were reminded that they are only one part of a public of many colors.

But today, as columnist Claude Lewis has pointed out, that public is being eroded:

> It is increasingly clear that nothing else will be as effective as the street demonstration. When the demonstrations were going on all over the nation on a daily basis, there were few riots and much progress. But today, without the marches for justice and equality, little or nothing seems to be going on. Among blacks those old feelings of hopelessness, helplessness, frustration and even despair are beginning to return. Some black leaders, unwilling to publicly predict return to rioting as a means of moving white America, are whispering about such dire possibilities in private.[4]

When we are reduced to "whispering in private" the chances for violence increase, for in private we can feel neither the limits nor the potentials which become evident in public life. Whispering in private is an image of pressure hissing toward an explosion. Public protest reduces the chances of violence, partly because it allows an open venting of angry feelings, partly because it puts pressure for change on the attitudes, practices and policies which give rise to the anger. As long as people are acting in public it is a sign of hope—for such action reflects the belief that there is a public to address, a public which will eventually respond. The consternation some Americans felt in the sixties when people were marching in the streets is nothing compared to the consternation we should feel today when public problems remain but the action has gone underground. We are living on the lid of a pressure cooker with a broken valve, and if we imagine otherwise we are living in a fool's paradise. The church needs to find ways of renewing the public by returning the action to the public streets.

Not all street action need be aimed at protesting injustice. We can help renew the public life by using the streets to celebrate the achievements and promise of our life together. This is what happens on the Fourth of July when the public gathers to recall its history and its founding vision. The church, with some imagination and a sense of sacred history, could find days even more appropriate for celebrations which help create a public.

There are other actions which can help reclaim the streets for public life—block parties, for example. When a street is cordoned off, refreshments provided, music and games offered by the neighbors to each other, and people are given an excuse to mingle for a few hours on a summer evening, then the street takes on new and more hospitable meaning. Do it often enough and that street becomes a place where people pass each other with warm memories and hopeful expectations rather than unawareness and suspicion.

Craft and art fairs in the streets have much the same effect—they give strangers an excuse for mixing and, in the process, establish the fact that the streets can build community as well as carry traffic. An art or craft fair has a couple of other interesting features, too. The artist's work is done in private, but the fair brings it into public; as we inspect a work of art we are invited to connect our subjective world with another's, and a public is being formed. Art in public allows us to feel related to each other, to find that vital link which helps create the public life.

But the major action which shapes the character of public streets is conducted by speculators, realtors, banks, and construction firms. When an urban park is rezoned for commercial use and a high-rise office building is built upon the site, the public life suffers. When "urban renewal" drives families and small businesses out of an area in order to construct condominiums, the public life is diminished. Whenever open space for people to mingle is converted into more "efficient" (i.e., profitable) use, the public life is strangled in the process.

Most of us are ignorant about machinations of this sort, or feel powerless to do much about them. But the church can influence this kind of action if it takes time to learn how it happens and why. The church needs to be aware of the zoning boards and planning commissions which decide how city spaces will be used. The church can maintain a presence before these groups, pressing for uses of space which will encourage the public life. To do so, we need to understand the logic of speculation, to see how often decisions are made in service of profit rather than human need. We need to learn ways of fighting such decisions, not with appeals to idealism but with public actions which make the decisions unprofitable. Demonstrations, media campaigns, and boycotts are all tactics for reducing the profit to be made by acts against the public. Not only do such tactics help defeat raw commercialism, but they also build a public as they are employed, for they require people to come together on matters of common concern. If the church could hold up a vision of multiple and well-integrated uses of city space—and find the means of making the vision muscular—it would have made a major contribution to the renewal of public life.

5

In addition to symbolic space and physical space, there is also institutional space. The church could do much to develop institutions which offer space for public experience.

Just as the physical design of our cities tends to keep us apart, so the way our institutions are organized tends to divide and isolate us. For example, young people are separated from the grandparent's generation by families which exclude the elderly, and by institutions such as schools and nursing homes which keep children on one track and the elderly on another, seldom allowing the tracks to converge. The institutions of segregation keep blacks and whites apart. Hospitals and mental institutions isolate sick people from those who are well. In all of these ways the public life is defeated just as surely as if we had built concrete walls between portions of the population. We need to find ways for existing institutions to connect groups rather than isolate them, and we need to invent new institutions which will create connections where none exist.

In many communities—especially our suburbs—there is only one institution which reaches throughout the population, only one which has a chance of drawing a public to it. I mean the public school. This was the case in a community where I once lived, a "bedroom suburb" of a large urban center. The physical area contained a nice mix of ages, races, and income levels, but had no facilities for public gathering, only row upon row of houses and apartment buildings where people lived their private lives. The school served to bring us together, and then only for the occasional

PTA meeting or student musical. The school was the sole institution capable of attracting a public (and even that "public" was limited to adults with school-age children).

Then word came that the Board of Education was planning to close the school; the facility was old and the number of school-aged children in the area had been dropping for several years. Some of us saw that the loss of the school would devastate our sense of community, so we organized to defend the school not simply as an educational institution but as an institution which builds a public. Our strategy was not based simply on the needs of our children, for here the Board of Education had statistics on its side. Instead, we argued that the school could and should be used for a variety of community functions; that its continuation would be justified if it served not only the children but also other community groups. For example, its kitchen facilities could be used to prepare hot lunches for invalids and elderly people in the area. Unused rooms in the school could serve as offices for certain public services— welfare, legal aid, mental health—or be rented to voluntary associations. The gymnasium could be made available for political meetings, or used for speakers and films with community appeal.

In all of these ways, the school becomes a public crossroad. As people pass through it in pursuit of various interests and needs, they grow aware of one another as coparticipants in the public. If we could use our school buildings for such purposes, the schools might benefit as well. At the moment, these vital institutions suffer from a lack of public interest and/or confidence. If school facilities served the public more widely, the result might be a more constructive public attitude toward school problems. And practical difficulties such as vandalism might be reduced if school buildings were in more constant use. Somehow we must learn that the actual presence of the public, the ebb and flow of public life itself, can mitigate problems which cannot be touched by the abstraction called "public concern."

Sometimes we need to go beyond the redesign of existing institutions to invent new ones. That may sound like an overwhelming task to those who have never tried it, but it is not. Let me illustrate from personal experience.

I once lived in a suburb which lacked any form of local community government. Though the community was a large one, it was governed by a county council which was distant, both physically and psychologically, from the people. Residents felt isolated from one another, incapable of dealing corporately and creatively with community problems. A few of us in the church gathered to think about the problem and realized that in order to call out a public, to evoke a sense of our mutual responsibilities, some sort of new institution was needed, an institution where people could meet, discuss community issues, decide on priorities, and gain access to resources for action. That is, we needed an institution which could perform some of the public-building functions of local government. After considerable conversation, we developed the idea of establishing a "community foundation."

This foundation would have an endowment fund which, wisely invested, would generate a given amount of money each year. Residents could come to the foundation seeking funds for projects aimed at bringing the community together; decisions about which projects to fund would be made by the foundation's board, a group consisting of persons drawn from all segments of the community. Thus, one person might ask for $200 to finance a block party. Another might seek $2000 to underwrite a drama-in-the-parks program during the summer months. We hoped that a public would be formed not only through projects such as these, but through the very processes of the foundation itself—assembling the board, inviting the community to think about its needs, encouraging individuals and groups to develop projects to meet those needs, debating priorities for the allocation of funds, and seeking to enlarge the endowment by persuading donors of the community's potential.

To find an organizational base from which to launch the foundation, we turned to the only institution besides the school in which large numbers of suburbanites are involved—the church. We brought together a coalition of some twenty congregations whose ministers shared our concern and, with them, developed a strategy. Our first step was to design an action-research project which involved eight or ten persons from each congregation conducting door-to-door interviews at a sampling of homes in the community. The interviewers learned much about people's perceptions of the community's needs. But more important, the interviewing process took these normally isolated church members out into the community, into homes and lives they had never seen, where they could begin to develop a sense for the public and its life.

As a result, the research process yielded not only information. It also created in each congregation a cadre of eight to ten people (the interviewers) who saw the need for a new institution to help cultivate the public, a cadre ready to support the next step—the request that each congregation put up enough money to finance a three year effort at getting a community foundation established. In the end, each church pledged an average of $1000 a year, for a total of $20,000 a year over a three year period. With that money we were able to organize a board, incorporate, hire a director, and begin the process of building an endowment.

I am telling this story to indicate that inventing a new institution is possible. You simply do it one step at a time. In a society such as ours, with so many institutions caught in self-maintenance rather than public service, we need to invent new institutional spaces in which a public can gather. I believe that the church has special opportunities, and obligations, to do so. Because of its general respectability in the community, the church can provide the new institution with an aura of trust and goodwill which might otherwise take years to earn. With its nonprofit status, the church can incorporate new projects into its own programs and receive tax-exempt donations on their behalf, thus making it unnecessary for the project to incorporate itself. In the case of the community foundation, it seemed wise to seek independent incorporation, so lawyers from two congregations volunteered their services. Here is another resource the church can offer—the technical skills of its members which are often needed to help new institutions get started. And congregations often have unused physical space which can be shared with new institutions; the community foundation was housed in a spare classroom in one of the sponsoring churches. In all of these ways, the church can help renew the public by fostering new institutions which offer public space.

6

Finally, since the church has always understood education to be one of its most important functions, I want to show how educational programs can offer space for strangers to meet, for a public to be formed. I do not mean the internal educational programs of the church, Sunday school and the like; I have already suggested theological themes which might be taught in those settings as a contribution to public life. Here, I want to suggest ways of taking "religious" education into the public realm where nonmembers can be reached and public awareness aroused. Again, I want to speak from personal experience.

I once worked as a community organizer in a suburb which had been exclusively white and middle class, but was rapidly becoming home for a growing number of blacks, Latinos, and other minorities. The problem, as my colleagues and I saw it, was to help white residents become accustomed to and comfortable with these changes, to help them see both the inevitability and the benefits of a pluralistic society. We wanted especially to fight against the "white flight" which would create just another ghetto.

One of our responses was to design a series of educational events called "Living Room Seminars" on the topic "Coping with Community Change." Working through churches, we would identify an individual or family who had a constructive concern about these problems. We asked these people if they would be willing to invite ten or fifteen neighbors into their home for a seminar that met one evening a week for eight weeks; we would provide leadership for the meetings and take care of all the logistics. To our delight, many people quickly agreed, perhaps because the isolation of suburban life made them yearn for contact with their neighbors and for the stimulation of new ideas.

The seminar had three stages. First, we asked members of the group to assess their own resistance or openness to the changes going on in their community. Most people, of course, will claim that they are completely open-minded, so to take us a step further we had participants answer a psychological questionnaire intended to measure "open- and closed-mindedness." No questionnaire can reveal all the nuances of a person's mind, but the one we used was good enough to stimulate self-reflection and enable people to see beyond their ideal self-images. With the questionnaire, and with the development of group trust, most participants were able to express their own uneasiness with the strangers who were moving in around them—and to experience some healing in that honesty.

In a second stage of the seminar, we explored the conditions under which people are empowered to deal with change in an open and creative way rather than becoming brittle, reactionary, and self-defeating. We looked at our own autobiographies, looking for points at which we were able to adapt to new circumstances and trying to identify the factors that made adaptation possible (e.g., the support of friends, or a strong sense of God's presence in our lives). We also read the writings of scholars who have studied how people move from a traditional situation into the radically new (e.g., Margaret Mead's *New Lives for Old*).

In the third stage, we asked the group to choose at least one of those factors which enable people to cope creatively with change, and to design and implement a project which would help make that factor available to others in their community. In fact, we insisted that the seminar could not end until the group had taken some part of what they had learned about coping with change and made it available to others.

One seminar, for example, decided that people cope better with change when they know each other than they do when they feel isolated. So, to enhance the sense of relatedness in their own neighborhood, they dreamed up a "catalogue" of personal skills and resources which neighbors could share with one another. Members of the seminar spent several weeks going door to door to collect the information, soliciting small donations to get the material mimeographed, and then distributing the results to every home in a six-block area. In the very process of putting the catalogue together they were building a public, and the catalogue itself gave neighbors a way of continuing to relate publicly as they called upon each other for various kinds of help.

This kind of "religious education" has no explicit theological content. But it does fulfill the root meaning of both words. It is educational in that it draws us out of ourselves into public relationships; it is religious in that it helps rebind our life together. Here is yet another way for the church in mission to help renew our public life.

9

Hope for the Public
Private Contemplation and the Public Congregation

1

In the course of writing this book and talking with others about it, I have often been asked how one can hope for the renewal of America's public life. Our corporate vision of the public is dim. Seldom in our daily routine do we have significant experience with strangers. The physical spaces and social processes in which the public might come to know itself have disappeared, dwindled, or been given over to other ends. We are surrounded by evidence of disunity, and whatever hope of unity we may cling to seems far off and even illusory.

Without a public life, problems which require public solutions multiply apace. We have a "public policy" permitting first-strike action with nuclear weapons, but no public to call the government back to sanity. Racism and sexism and class injustice demand a public response, but are themselves symptoms of public disintegration. We face problems of scarcity which only a public can solve, but the scarcities themselves seem to diminish the public even further.

So it is not surprising that our culture supports spiritual and political forms of self-centeredness. When our outward life is so fragmented; when the society seems incapable of sustaining, let alone generating, symbols of wholeness; when our very sense of self is threatened by conditions which deny the value of persons; then it is only natural that people will fold into themselves in a desperate though misguided bid to protect whatever sense of self remains. Viewing this process one is tempted to see it as a vicious circle or downward spiral from which there is no relief: the public deteriorates and becomes less supportive of the individual, causing individuals to turn ever more inward, thus allowing the public to decline even further.

In the midst of all this, what are the sources of hope? Some will find hope in programs for social action, thus reflecting the historic American bias that any problem can be taken care of by "doing something" (and it sometimes seems not to matter what, exactly, is done; the doing itself is a sort of therapy). Since the preceding four chapters suggest things the church can do to help renew the public's life, it might be thought that I too regard action as the grounds of hope. Not so. Though action is promising, important, even obligatory for Christians, it is not the final word. I am too mindful of the sixties, perhaps, a decade in which all hope was pinned to the human capacity to create a new heaven on earth, a decade whose dreams by now have been thoroughly dashed. In fact, the disillusionments of the sixties are partly responsible for the unhealthy forms of inwardness which overtook us in the past decade.

2

My hope, as a Christian, is grounded not in our own ability to solve problems but in God's love, God's justice, God's promise of fidelity to us. That promise, as we have seen, is the promise of reconciliation, a kingdom in which strangers will know themselves to be as one, a kingdom of which the church and the public life can be harbingers or foretastes. Though we may not be faithful to God, God will be faithful to us: that is the true source of Christian hope in a broken world.

What God requires of those who call on God's name is responsive servanthood. God wishes to act in and through us, so Christian hope does not relieve men and women of responsibility. But Christian faith compels us to re-vision the nature of our responsibility. We are not primarily responsible for shrewd analysis of problems, for strategic selection of means, for maximizing the chances of success. We are primarily responsible for turning to God, for attempting to know and do God's will. That will may lead us into actions which are not shrewd, strategic, or successful, as the life of Jesus suggests. But as Jesus' life demonstrates, human action which is faithful to God's will can have transforming effect.

This understanding of hope can help us break the circle of despair which sees the inward turn of American culture leading to further public deterioration. For if we are asked to know and do God's will, then inward searching—in the form of prayer and contemplation—can contain hope for the public. Properly understood, the inward turn need not lead us away from the public realm but will take us more deeply into it. Properly understood, the interior journey will take us not into isolation and individualism, but into a more profound sense of our human unity, our oneness in God. In fact, with the outward disintegration of our public life, it may be that inward experience will become the primary arena in which the reality of the human community can once again be felt and symbolized.

If we are to know hope in God's will, then inward quest is necessary, for it is inwardly, in the stillness of prayer and contemplation, that God's word is most often clearly heard. If we are to touch again the root reality of human unity the inward quest is necessary, because the God who occupies the heart of our true self is the God at the heart of all other selves. And if our public action is not to lead to burn-out and despair, the inward quest is necessary once more, for it is inwardly that we renew the wellsprings of faith which sustain action, even action which does not "succeed."

Perhaps the most important ministry the church can have in the renewal of public life is a "ministry of paradox": not to resist the inward turn of American spirituality on behalf of effective public action, *but to deepen and direct and discipline that inwardness in the light of faith* until God leads us back to a vision of the public and to faithful action on the public's behalf. A ministry of paradox should be familiar to us, for that phrase characterizes Jesus' own ministry: "He who finds his life will lose it, but he who loses his life for my sake will find it". (Matt. 10:34). That kind of thinking may not be shrewd, strategic, or successful, but it is full of truth and faith, and those are the criteria of Christian action.

To have a ministry in the full power of paradox, we need to overcome our habitual dualism, our way of seeing polarities as contradictions rather than two ends of a dynamic tension which can work together in a powerful whole. Our dualism leads us to believe that contemplation and action are opposites, alternative ways of living, choices which have to be made. But the fact is that they are two poles of paradox, no more in opposition than breathing in and breathing out; and when we attempt to have one without the other we suffocate and die. If we are to renew our outward action by deepening our inward quest, we must first learn to see the inner and outer as two halves of the whole.

It should be clear that contemplation and action are at least complementary; that contemplation can serve to clarify our action; that action can bear the fruits of contemplation. But there is an even more profound unity between the two, which we can see in those moments when action becomes a kind of contemplation and contemplation becomes a kind of action. When a person takes an act of conscience—refusing to pay war taxes, for example—that action opens up the hidden structures of reality in ways that detached observation never could. The tax resister is able to contemplate truths about self and society which are not visible from an unengaged, business-as-usual stance. Then there are times when the very presence of a self steeped in contemplation exerts a kind of action, rippling the surrounding waters in ways which influence external events. Jesus was no activist by contemporary standards; he established no protest committees, nor did he try to seize institutional power. But his very presence, a presence made whole by prayer and faith in God, was enough to shake empires.

3

If the church is to deepen, direct, and discipline the inward life which so many people find compelling, we must first catch a vision of community which supports the solitude that makes authentic inwardness possible. That image of community will seem strange and distorted to some, for our dualism leads us to think of solitude and community as polar opposites. We have seen this dichotomy before; it is the same one we make between private and public life. But it is false. Solitude and community, like prayer and action, are two halves of a whole, incomplete without one another. Dietrich Bonhoeffer knew whereof he spoke when he said, "Let him who cannot be alone beware of community" and "Let him who is not in community beware of being alone."[1]

Perhaps it is self-evident why community will be difficult for the woman or man who does not know how to be alone. Community can weary us with its continual encounters and relentless demands, can pull us too far off center to build enduring relations with others. We need solitude to help us sustain community life.

But it may not be so evident why solitude will be difficult for us if we are not in community. After all, many people turn to solitude precisely because community seems to have failed them; the inward life often begins as a last resort for people who feel let down by outward relationships. There is nothing "wrong" with that; in fact, it is probably inevitable that serious spiritual searching must await that moment when a person realizes that all external props and comforts are unreliable and will eventually fall away. But such a search, if it is not rewoven into community, can easily lead not to solitude with God but to loneliness with one's self. And such loneliness can lead us to make the self into a god, as many have done today, an idolatry which results from the simple fact that isolated people need something to cling to, and lacking anything else they embrace themselves.

Our inward searching might take quite a different turn if the church could become a community which actively supports and guides people in their solitude. Suppose that the church were to affirm, vocally and vigorously, that time spent in solitary prayer and contemplation is just as valuable to the church's mission as time spent meeting with committees or preparing pot-luck suppers. Suppose the church were to say that all members need to spend some time in solitary prayer, and that some members may be specially called to such a life in lieu of more conventional involvements. Suppose the church were to offer people instruction or guidance for spending time in solitude, teaching people how to pray contemplatively. Suppose the church in its corporate worship were to recall the solitary life of its members, to pray for their nuture and support. Suppose the church were to hold before its members the witness of a long, historic procession of men and women of prayer who affirm that God's will is known within us, inwardly to be found.

With such supports, people would be helped to find God rather than loneliness in their solitary lives. Without such supports, the typical congregation is likely to foster neither solitude nor community but some sort of collective busyness which lies in between. For people who emerge from solitude with personal strength in the presence of God also emerge with a capacity for true community, for relations of endurance and fidelity mediated by the God in our midst.

Thomas Merton once said, "I owe it to others to be alone. When I am alone they are not they but my own true self." By "true self" Merton meant the self made true in God, the God who is encountered at the depths of solitary experience. If the church could be a community which supports solitude, people might be less likely to experience the loneliness which results in idolatry of self. If the church could be a community which supports solitude, that solitude would lead us back into community and back into the public life, where "they are not they, but my own true self." Such a solitude-in-community would renew in us the vision and strength from which faithful public action can flow.

4

If the church is to be a community which supports its members' solitude, it must also be a community in which the fruits of individual prayer and contemplation can be shared. Here again we encounter our habitual dualism: personal prayer is private, corporate worship is public, and never the two shall meet. And here is another reason why the inward life of our time sometimes leads us not toward the will of God but into self-serving fantasies of our own: the private is always subject to distortion—it needs the checking and balancing of public exposure and accountability. We stand a better chance of distinguishing God's will from our own if we share our private prayer in public, a sharing which is made impossible when we isolate private quest from corporate worship.

The fact is that the inward quest will bring us into contact with spirits of all kinds, not the Holy Spirit alone: "Beloved, do not believe in every spirit, but test the spirits to see whether they are of God; for many false prophets have gone out into the world" (I John 4:1). The spirits of greed and division and power and hatred are as much alive in us and our world as is the Spirit of justice and love. When we enter the world of contemplative stillness it is not always clear whose word we are hearing; and even if we know, we may still find some demonic word more attractive than the word of God. Every inward quest, every form of prayer and contemplation, needs to invoke the capacity for discernment—of good from evil, of true from false. And though discernment yields to no handy "how to do it" rules, it is clear that it happens in part as we share our prayer within the community of faith.

But how seldom this happens in most congregations. The fact is that most "public worship" is not a chance for individuals to "go public" with their private prayer. It is an actor-audience situation, with the bulk of the communication flowing from the pulpit to the congregation. How seldom do the gathered people have a chance to say and pray what is on their hearts and minds—out loud, in front of one another. And there is reason for this, the same reason we are so squeamish about the public life itself. We are afraid of expressing ourselves before others, afraid of the correction which might come, afraid too of what others might reveal to us, of the obligations which might befall us as we listen. As long as we worship solely within the context of highly structured liturgies, as long as a few trained (and sometimes constrained) people have near-total control over what is uttered in church, we will never face the challenges involved in knowing why people are praying, what they are praying for, what kind of response they think they are getting—or whether they believe in prayer at all!

For all the obvious strengths of structured liturgical worship (its qualities of historic rememberance, of time-tested teaching, of continuity with a great community of faith) such worship can also give people words to hide behind. But liturgical or not, worship too often allows people to hide behind the person of the pastor. Clearly, we often "personalize" the life of the congregation just as we have "personalized" our public life—by organizing it around the personalities of the leaders. In the typical church, the pastor prays for the people, speaks for the people, and is often expected to act for the people as well. Our intimacy with the pastor and his or her spirituality makes things "feel like church." But when we are challenged to make the church real by speaking, praying, and acting for ourselves and with each other, we grow fearful of the consequences of projecting our personalities on that public screen, of having to receive the projections of others. It is much more comfortable to let the pastor's personality be the pivot-point of our community life. But as we allow that to happen, we simply mirror the problem with our public life at large, and we prevent the congregation from becoming a vehicle to carry us toward public concern and involvement.

We need to understand that the life of the church is not to be organized around anyone's personality—the pastor's or our own. It is, instead, to revolve around the person, the Word, and the will of God, as those are received and manifested in our own lives, however imperfectly. Indeed, we can be sure that any one person's grasp of God's will is going to be imperfect, for each of us is a mere fragment of the whole. This is precisely why we need to "go public" with our prayer and contemplation. Only as individual understandings of God's will are compared, contrasted, and interwoven with each other can we begin to move toward the wholeness which God intends for us, the wholeness of the entire body of Christ.

So we need, quite literally, to put private prayer in the context of public worship. The congregation should not only offer instruction in prayer, courses to acquaint members with the traditions and disciplines of devotion. The congregation should also offer members occasions and encouragements to pray aloud in each other's presence, to share the experience of prayer in each other's lives.

Churches with highly structured liturgies could offer more periods of open and spontaneous prayer within the formal worship. Better still, such congregations could offer small group experiences in prayer, grounded perhaps in Bible study, as a supplement to the liturgical services. And beyond the times of formal worship, every church should help its members carry prayer into other occasions in its corporate life, especially those occasions when decisions are being made about the use of the community's resources, about directions for church mission.

In all of this, the congregation must encourage members to develop a corporate discipline of mutual guidance in prayer. It is not enough simply to pray together. We must also learn to reflect on our shared experience of prayer, to ask each other probing and caring questions, to share divergent experiences with prayer, to drop the plumb lines of Scripture and tradition and the whole church into our gathered midst. To put it in a phrase, the congregation which would truly "go public," which would ground its outward action in the discernment of spirits, must become a community of mutual spiritual guidance.

5

Spiritual guidance and the discernment of spirits are concepts familiar to Catholic and Orthodox Christians, but they have an alien sound to many Protestant ears. Protestantism has placed such heavy emphasis on the capacity of the believer to discern God's will for him or herself that the idea of anyone else attempting to guide that process sounds heretical. Yet at its core, Protestantism has always affirmed one source of spiritual guidance—the Scripture—and Scripture itself is in part the story of guidance received and tested by the community of faith. There is no necessary opposition between Protestant principles and the concept of corporate guidance in prayer.

Today, even in the Protestant churches, there is a growing sense of the need for spiritual guidance. Protestant seminaries, like their Roman Catholic and Anglican counterparts, are now offering preparation for clergy in the traditions and disciplines of prayer, with the result that more and more ministers take up their work ready to counsel with people who want to deepen their inward relation with God. This is all to the good, but it does not go far enough. Reliance on the minister for spiritual guidance merely reinforces the clergy-centered pattern of too much congregational life. For the sake of the church and its mission (and for the sake of an overburdened clergy as well) we need to make spiritual guidance and discernment a community enterprise. In such a community, the minister will surely offer leadership, and Scripture and tradition will surely be invoked. But such a community will understand that it diminishes the power of Christ's body on earth by failing to function collectively, attempting to discern the Spirit's movement in *this* problem, at *this* moment, with *these* people. The English poet Sydney Carter overstates the case, but still provides us with a healthy challenge and corrective, when he says:

> Your holy hearsay
> is not evidence
> give me the good news
> in the present tense.

I have stressed the importance of communal guidance first because the body as a whole has powers of discernment which its members in isolation lack. Each of us needs the community of faith to help find clues for faithfulness in an often bewildering world. But there is another reason, as well. Our discernment of God's will is incomplete until we have done God's will. And action, though it is undertaken by individuals, always needs community support and encouragement.

We need to learn the lessons of the past two decades of church social action. During this time, the social witness of the mainline churches in America has been flawed and often undermined or undone by the fact that it did not emerge from a corporate testing of direction, a collective sense of mission. It came, instead, from the prophetic insight of a few who were in a position to control the resources and the official voice of the church. The fact that one may agree with much of that prophecy, as I do (eg., that which has called us to account for our complicity in racial injustice, or in the exploitation of third-world peoples) is beside the point. The point is that a prophet is not one who manipulates the machinery of the church toward self-appointed goals, but one who calls the church to repentence under the judgment of God, who tries to move the community in truth. The gathered people of God—however slow and unseeing—must be led together toward a vision of peace and justice if the church is fully to engage the needs of a suffering world.

That lesson has been partially learned in recent years; it is not uncommon for Christians to claim that prophetic leaders must stay close to the church in order to strengthen their political base and gain access to a larger pool of resources. There is practical wisdom in such counsel, for the work of reconciliation is too large to be done by individuals: it requires a community effort. But there is danger in this counsel as well, for it tends to make the church more a political tool than an instrument of God's will. I am arguing that the prophet must stay close to the church for reasons more spiritual than political. The prophet's discernment of the spirits must be tested within the community of prayer; only as this is done will we know the truth of the prophecy. This will make the prophet's life one of struggle and anguish, for the community as a whole can be blind and resistant. But the biblical record suggests that such has always been the plight of prophecy. Yet Scripture also teaches that when the community comes to recognize the prophet as the voice of God, a great power is unleashed on earth, a power not of politics but of faithfulness, the faithfulness of the body of Christ. The church today, as always, will generate faithful corporate action only as it cultivates the capacity for common prayer in which Christian action touches its ground and its hope.

6

I began this book with a story about Thomas Merton, and I return to him now at the close. It is appropriate to do so, for the Merton who emerged from a long inward search to discover the public at the corner of Fourth and Walnut in Louisville was also the Merton whose inward search was guided and formed by a strong community of faith. Far from being a seeker and prophet in isolation from the church, Merton was immersed in and nurtured by a religious tradition and community. He often found himself in tension and conflict with that community, a fact which brought much anguish to his life. But he stayed with it, speaking to the community and listening in humility even when he was rejected—and in that tension his prayer and prophecy grew in power.

That power, of course, was God's gift to him, a gift which seemed to multiply as Merton stayed faithful to God's broken body on earth. And through that faithfulness, the pain and brokenness in Merton's life became infused with joy, a joy which spilled over the walls of monastery and church into a vision of the whole public world.

Late in his life Merton wrote an essay called "The Street is for Celebration," and I wonder if the memory of Fourth and Walnut Streets kindled him as he wrote. His subject is the city streets, and he begins by facing without blinking the ways in which those public spaces have been turned into battlegrounds of division and conflict and fear by spirits which are not of God. He would have understood my New York City taxi driver who said, "You never know who's getting into the cab, so it's a little dangerous." But with the cabbie, Merton then sings a hymn of praise and hope—the praise of a God who has promised to reconcile us to one another, the hope of redeeming those public spaces through corporate celebration:

> Celebration is not noise. It is not a spinning head. It is not just individual kicks. It is the creation of a common identity, a common consciousness. Celebration is everybody making joy . . . Celebration is when we let joy make itself out of our love . . . Celebration is crazy; the craziness of not having submitted even though "they," "the others," the ones who make life impossible, seem to have all the power. Celebration is the beginning of confidence, therefore of power . . . They with their gold have turned our lives into rubble . . . But we with our love will set our lives on fire and turn the rubble back into gold. This time the gold will have real worth . . . It will be the infinite value of human identity flaming up in a heart that is confi-

dent in loving . . . The Bible tells us that in the end it will be like
that again, in a city of pure celebration . . . One day, you'll see![2]

In Merton's words we catch a vision of a public life transformed
by God's promise to us. In the experience behind those words we
see the process by which that vision comes into being. It is a process
of inward search, deepened, disciplined, and directed by the community of faith; a search which leads us to the God in whom we
are all made one; a God who brings us outward into "the company
of strangers" with courage to face its powers of conflict and division because we are aflame with God's promise of justice and love.
Here is hope for the public. One day, we'll all see.

Notes

Chapter 1

1. Søren Kierkegaard, *The Present Age* (New York: Harper Torchbooks, 1962), p. 63.
2. "An Open Letter: The Public and its Education" (Philadelphia: Board of Christian Education, United Presbyterian Church U.S.A., 1969), p. 14.
3. Vincent Harding, "Out of the Cauldron of Struggle: Black Religion and the Search for a New America" (*Soundings* LXI:3, Fall 1978): 350–51.
4. Thomas Merton, *Conjectures of a Guilty Bystander* (New York: Image Books, 1968), pp. 156–57.

Chapter 2

1. John Dewey, *The Public and its Problems* (Denver: Alan Swallow, 1927), p. 185
2. Robert Bellah, "Commentary and Proposed Agenda: The Normative Framework for Pluralism in America" (*Soundings* LXI:3, Fall 1978): 356.
3. Richard Titmus, *The Gift Relationship* (New York: Pantheon Books, 1971), p. 157.
4. Quoted in the newsletter of the Wellspring Mission of the Church of the Savior, Washington, D.C. I have been unable to find its original source.
5. William Severini Kowinski, "The Malling of America" (*New Times,* May 1978): 43, 46, 54.
6. *Ibid.:* 36.
7. Richard Sennett, *The Fall of Public Man* (New York: Alfred A. Knopf, 1977), p. 259.

Chapter 3

1. Thomas Merton, *The Collected Poems of Thomas Merton* (New York: New Directions Books, 1977), p. 383.
2. Robert E. Meagher, "Strangers at the Gates" (*Parabola* II:4): 11.
3. Henri Nouwen, *Reaching Out* (Garden City, N. Y: Doubleday, 1975), p. 51.

Chapter 4

1. Richard Sennett, *The Fall of Public Man*, p. 337.
2. Christopher Lasch, "The Narcissist Society" (*The New York Review of Books*, 30 September 1976): 15.
3. Paul Goodman, *Growing Up Absurd* (New York: Vintage Books, 1960), p. 97.
4. Philip Rieff, *The Triumph of the Therapeutic* (New York: Harper Torchbooks, 1968).
5. Christopher Lasch, "The Narcissist Society" (*The New York Review of Books*, 30 September, 1976): 15.
6. Peter Marin, "The New Narcissism" (*Harper's Magazine,* October 1975): 56.
7. Alexis deTocqueville, *Democracy in America* (New York: Harper & Row, 1966).
8. Quoted in Peter Marin, "The New Narcissism" (*Harper's Magazine,* October 1975): 56.

Chapter 5

1. David Potter, *People of Plenty* (Chicago: University of Chicago Press, 1954).
2. Colin Turnbull, *The Mountain People* (New York: Simon and Schuster, 1972).

Chapter 6

1. Richard Sennett, *The Fall of Public Man*, p. 260.
2. E. F. Schumacher, *Small is Beautiful* (New York: Harper & Row, 1975), pp. 97–98.

Chapter 8

1. Thomas Merton, *Seasons of Celebration* (New York: Farrar, Straus and Giroux, 1965), p. 3.
2. Neal Peirce, "He Soured on Shopping Centers" (*The Philadelphia Inquirer,* 23 October 1978): 7–A.
3. William Severini Kowinski, "The Malling of America" (*New Times,* May 1978): 34.
4. Claude Lewis, "Rights Slowdown" (*The Philadelphia Bulletin,* 15 January 1979): editorial page.

Chapter 9

1. Dietrich Bonhoeffer, *Life Together* (New York: Harper & Row, 1954), p. 77.

2. Thomas Merton, *Love and Living* (New York: Farrar, Straus and Giroux, 1979), pp. 53, 51.